from a coastal kitchen

from a coastal kitchen

hancock house

ISBN 0-88839-071-8

Copyright © 1980 Reid, Lee

Canadian Cataloging in Publication Data

Reid, Lee. 1946-
    From a Coastal Kitchen

    ISBN 0-88839-071-8 pa.
    1. Coastal Kitchen - British Columbia.
2. British Columbia - Social Life and Customs. I. Title.
TX715.R44   641.59711   C80-091189-X

Printed in Canada

Published by
HANCOCK HOUSE PUBLISHERS LTD.
#10 Orwell St. North Vancouver, B.C. V7J 3K1

Contents

Jams & Jellies

Seafood

Meats

Cooked Vegetable Dishes

Desserts

Acknowledgments

With love and appreciation —
for my artist, Barb Wood, who created all the drawings,
for my pal Beth Erickson, whose professional photography
adorns this book.

Foreword

"We spent one of the best weeks a father and son can have with John and Lee Reid at their fishing resort in Knight Inlet. Early mornings, late nights, rain — drizzle — fog — all part of the price but what a reward to come 'home' to Lee's kitchen afloat and sit down to some of the best, most delicious and truly innovative dishes I have experienced over the past thirty-two years. This is a book to use and to treasure and for Andy and I — it's a constant reminder that the salmon are waiting in Lull Bay!"

Graham Kerr

The Galloping Gourmet

Sointula

Alert Bay   *Freshwater Bay*

Port McNeill

The Blow

Bones Bay

Crancroft

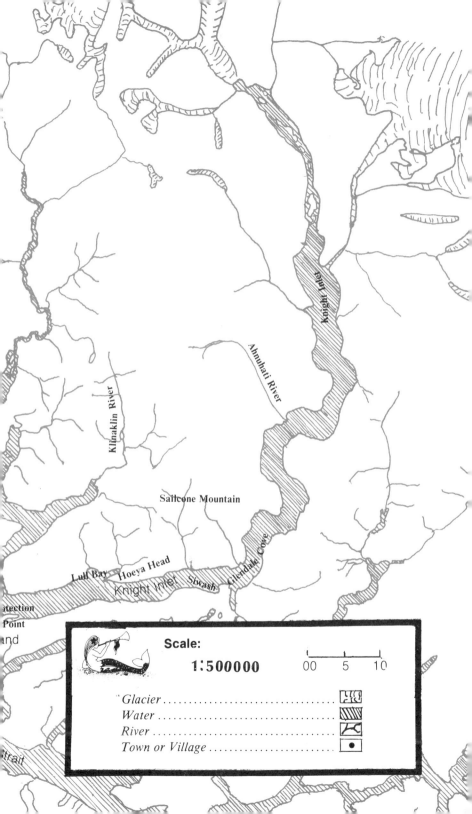

Knight Inlet

Ahnuhati River

Klinaklin River

Sailcone Mountain

Lull Bay   Hoeya Head   Siwash   Glendale Cove

Knight Inlet

tection
Point
nd

trait

Scale:

1:500000

00   5   10

Glacier .... 🏔
Water .... 🌊
River .... 🏞
Town or Village .... •

Introduction

Nine years ago, I couldn't have guessed that Knight Inlet would become our home. After all, we were educators: teachers and counselors, geared to a college or school career. We certainly loved the coast; had grown up on Vancouver Island; as kids, fished off Sidney and Sooke and Brentwood. But we didn't seriously consider even living on the coast until our Alaska trip. Our goals were freedom - to teach while traveling, and maybe to fit in a bit of fishing; a weekend boat trip now and then.

By summer 1970, we were tired of grad school; we wanted action! To explore the coast, living off seafoods; a boat excursion to Alaska! We crammed sleeping bags and Coleman stove into John's twenty-foot handbuilt tub, proceeded to puddlejump, salmon-fish, and leak in haphazard trek from Vancouver to Sechelt's oyster bed to Alert Bay. Here John introduced me to Knight Inlet - a deep, mountainous gash in the coast range. We camped beside a trout stream at Glendale Cove, surrounded by glacial ocean, killer whales, families of bald eagles, and the immense alive silence of the wilderness. I feasted off fried trout, feeling that Knight Inlet was "Home." On we pushed, to clam beds and Port Hardy. We showered in the ghost canneries and towns of Namu and Bella Bella. At Prince Rupert we waded over floors slimy with fishblood to reach baths at the cannery. Then on through a two-week diet of cockles - up the Alaska Panhandle to Skagway. This really challenged me to be creative with my cooking: an unending stream of "curried cockles," "cockle-chowder," "creamed cockles," "cockle hotcakes" and "scrambled cockles."

We were hooked! Now we *had* to live or work on or near the coast. And I determined to learn more about cooking. So we gambled. We built ourselves a tiny floating lodge on metal pontoons. We called her *The Aunt Molly*: our home and summer resort between teaching and travel.

Meanwhile we taught or lived in coast towns in the winters: Port McNeill, Sointula, Alert Bay; then for two years we taught English in Japan and Greece. Always, by summer, we'd return to Knight Inlet, impatient to tow our minute fishing resort up to Lull Bay. We couldn't wait!

Many of our repeat guests were becoming friends. They too loved the coast, having settled themselves in coastal Washington, Oregon, and California.

Increasingly, we liked the physical activity - boating and cooking - involved in a resort, and we preferred the freedom of working for ourselves. Although it seemed at most a "break even" business and a lot of hard work, we enjoyed the life.

Our resort slowly prospered. Guests came from Vancouver Island, the U.S. coast, Hawaii; then increasingly, from Saskatchewan, Alberta, Nebraska, Texas, Arizona, Idaho, Utah and even Maine and New York. Meanwhile, I experimented with international and gourmet cookery, with coast and local recipes and with guests' contributed favorites. As the resort grew, I built my own eclectic cooking style. I got to know the Johnstone Straits - Queen Charlotte Straits area, and its people.

Finally, we could afford to spend all our time in Knight Inlet. We left teaching for winters in the wilderness. Now we fish five summer months of each year in Lull Bay, then tow the lodge down Knight Inlet to harbor near Minstrel Island. Our hobby fishing resort has become our life.

To be honest, it's an isolated, yet worthwhile, life. You find that on the coast, as in the inlet, food and human companionship are vital. The sea - mountain aloneness generates a deep human need for companionship, laughter, and a sharing of experience and work.

With us, sports fishing and group meals provide this focus. Beyond us, in coast homes, people "get together" over home cooked meals and "potlucks" to trade music, advice, jokes, stories. They part feeling warmed, filled. Sharing meals means an exchange of care and friendship.

The Pacific country is reflected in its people: in their independence and practicality; in a physical, active approach to maintaining life. Communication is direct, sensible. Life means fishing, logging, crabbing, boat building and repairs, often with direct exchange of goods, such as fish for work. Life also consists of active day-to-day chores such as wood chopping, home maintaining, gardening, and clam digging. Often people shop and visit neighbors by boat, traveling long distances to the nearest home or store.

In this area, keeping food fresh over two or three weeks is normal. People "make do" on root vegetables until the next communal boat trip to the nearest town.

Appreciation of natural beauty shows, concretely, in the home crafts and artifacts casually placed in coast kitchens and living rooms: jewelry, pottery, macrame and weaving, woodcarving, ironwork and wood furniture; collections of antique Chinese bottles, Indian masks and beads. Much of the work is done, carefully and lovingly, by hand.

Aesthetically, most folk share an implicit love of nature, which is why they've chosen this area and way of life. The land's beauty, peace and wave-wind rhythms bring people closer to their own inner harmonies. Spiritually, one is struck with a sense of mystery and timelessness; of massive mountain life and clear, fragile light. From all viewpoints, the land's spirit and shadows soothe. Enchanted, people visit and settle, or return again and again to our resort. The inlet winds and mists penetrate their blood.

Many of my recipes are from coast folk, friends' and neighbors' good cooking. Many I've omitted because only local people have access to the ingredients. However, I do share with you some succulent memories in recipes like salal berry jelly, glazed wild boar and mussel bouillabaisse.

Most coast cooking, however, is basic, simple, and tasty. People boil or steam shellfish: clams, crab, prawns - all delicious dipped in melted butter. They bake, smoke or fry fish (mostly local salmon or cod). Chowders are also popular.

For this cookbook, I've collected some of the more unusual coastal recipes, using commonly available foods, and I've added international favorites from our friends and guests, plus my own creations. Among the recipes I've woven tales of local people, the flavor of this country and the lifestyle of a coast fishing resort.

Breakfast, Brunch &
Lunch Recipes

Mornings on the coast arrive slowly, pregnant with nature. Time poised. Growing energy of mountain, man, ocean, winds. Through thick mists, muted wave pulsations. Expanding quiet.

Dawn in the resort; I float into morning. A precious time. Resort, land, and I gather life.

Translucent light ripples.... Increasing natural melody: clam slurpings; stirrings, snortings and chuckles in the lodge; loons echoing soft loneliness to the scrapping humorous garble of crow families.

Sunlight warmth raises yeasty earth aromas. Puffs of seagulls. Birds, mists wraith out to sea. Whimsically, my mind creates and plays with the day's menu. Thuddings, rustles and ploddings of people into morning.

Time for guests to challenge the fishing and the weather. For coast people to start up their generators and their inner engines: the machinery of work day. For this unpredictable land to resist our routine habits of business or secure boredom. Time for me to drift down the stairs and bound into my kitchen. Glowing to translate morning into meals.

Mornings connect me to life. A time to share over the renewal of morning coffee.

15

John's a fishing genius. He instincts his way to where sneaky fish hide, intuits them into his net; by sheer experience, perseverance, skill and a sixth "fishing sense" he assures his boat of more and bigger fish.

John looks the fisherman part. Weathered and honest square face, Robinson Crusoe beard, perceptive brown eyes that respond to every subtlety of tide, current and wind. People trust his deep voice, air of assured power; and his dimples....

Without John the resort couldn't survive. He's our Knight Inlet multi-talented engineer. John keeps all our machines obedient: boat engines, generator, hot tub, marine toilets, dishwasher, water hose system to the land, freezers, fish smoker; he maintains and repairs them all. If the shower system plugs up with salamanders, everyone yells "help" for John... if the well runs dry, John's the one who patiently hacks his way through the bush, laying down hose to connect us with Lull Bay Creek... when, inevitably, the boats spring a leak, John expertly fibreglasses them... when we need wood for the fish smoker or our woodstove, John has energy to chop it. Amidst all this, he coordinates reservations by radio phone with Ruby, our Vancouver secretary, maintains our stock or bait, repairs our fishing gear, does the laundry for me on "changeover" days when we switch guests, keeps up his accounts, and, to escape it all, happily fishes nine to twelve hours a day.

John's a strong man who loves his work - the resort he's created.

Here's his favorite tart morning drink; uplifting juice for the returning fishermen:

Rindy Orange Juice

Serves 8 to 10

A tart, orange-filled juice to pique the palate before you serve breakfast or brunch. I make it up the night before so it has time to "marinate" in its own rind. People constantly request this simple recipe.

4 oz. ea.	2 pkgs. any brand orange-juice crystals (eg. I use Nabob *Sungold*, or *Tang* crystals)	*113 g ea.*
8 cups	cold water, including any leftover juice from canned fruits squeezed juice and chopped pulp of two medium oranges (reserve the rind)	*2 L*

finely grated rind of l¹½ to 2 oranges-
(add rind until juice is tart enough for you)
more sugar, if you prefer, to taste

Stir well. Combine ingredients in a 2 quart (8 to 10 cup) jug or container, chill overnight, or *at least* 2 hours, keep well-covered. *To Serve:* Shake or stir well before pouring, and enjoy!

Inlet Continental Coffee

Deep and strong. Tastes like Greek or French blend, which it partially is. There's nothing like 6 a.m. brew to wake guests up. Use a drip-pot - ours is aluminum. (This is *not* Mellita drip.) It's cheaper, because you combine regular commercial coffee with dark ground beans. I grind our own every morning for breakfast, but you can do this at your market.

1/3 measure fine or drip-ground dark (e.g. french or chocolate) roasted beans.
2/3 measure any drip or fine-ground commercial packaged coffee.
Combine the ground coffees in drip part of your pot.
Pour boiling water into top and let sit to drip through.
Stir before serving.
Re-heat to serve.

Hot Rum Or Whiskey

Serves 1

I make this up when chilled men return from fishing, at sunset.

1-2 heap-ing tsp.	butter	*5-10 mL*
1 heaping tsp.	brown sugar or more to taste	*5-10 mL*
	(or 3 tsps.15 mL honey)	
	1 whole clove	
	liberal pinch ground cinnamon	
	liberal pinch ground nutmeg	
	liberal pinch allspice	
2 huge tsps.	any commercial hot rum mix	*10 mL*
	(optional)	

Fill l/3 to l/4 of a large mug with dark rum, or rye whiskey. Add above ingredients and stir well. Pour in boiling water, stirring. Maybe add more booze - to taste. Serve immediately.

In my resort, I serve herbed fish cubes every morning as pre-breakfast appetizers. The guests fillet their smallest salmon and rush them to my kitchen.

Herbed Fish Cubes

Serves 4 to 6

Use at breakfast or as dinner hors d'oeuvres. Easy to prepare on your boat, on shore, or in a city kitchen. Crispy-fried strips or fillets of salmon or cod. Also good with fish roe, milt, or with leftover roast beef, raw kidney or liver.

My measures here are basically "palm of hand." I concoct the herb mix ahead of time, then marinate the fish or beef strips in evaporated milk. At serving time, I roll them in the herb-flour mixture, fry quickly in bacon fat, and serve hot on paper towels.

4 or more small fillets of cod or salmon:

Up to thirty minutes ahead of time prepare fillets by removing all skin and slicing in thin, finger-size strips, place in bowl and cover with evaporated milk. Stir. Bring to room temperature.

Herb Flour

2/3 cup	all-purpose flour (or more)	*200 mL*
2 tsp.	seasoning salt (or more or less to taste)	*10 mL*
1 to 2 tsp.	'fines herbs' (*Spice Islands* puts out a commercial blend of this)	*5-10 mL*
I/2 tsp.	dried leaf rosemary - (or more, to taste)	*2 mL*
I/2 tsp.	ginger powder - (or more, to taste)	*2 mL*
1 to 2 tsp.	*Coleman's* dried mustard powder	*5-10 mL*
1 tsp.	dried dill weed- (or more to taste)	*5 mL*

Combine ingredients in a bowl and stir well. You may need to double the ingredients if you run out before all fish is coated. This is easy to prepare ahead.

At serving time, melt bacon fat (enough to well-cover skillet bottom), roll strips in flour mix, fry quickly. Drain on paper towel and serve immediately.

Note: To use with roast beef or even thin slices of kidney or liver, proceed as above, but fry meats in butter for a richer taste.

Excellent as hot hors d'oevres for dinner or as a main course.

Homemade Yogurt

Thick and creamy. High protein energy during our active l6-hour days. Takes 6 to 10 hours to "jell." Although I prefer yogurt plain, you might not appreciate the taste of canned evaporated milk. In this case, stir in a 3 oz. (135 g)pkg. of fruit -flavored Jello into the warm freshly-made yogurt and allow it to set awhile longer before you chill it. Strawberry and peach are particularly tasty.

1 cup	canned evaporated milk	250 mL
1 cup	instant skim milk powder	250 mL
3 cups	medium-warm water	750 mL
3 heaping dessertspoons	any commercial brand of plain yogurt.	25 mL

I usually buy a large tub from our city supermarket (it lasts at least two weeks) as a "culture base" for my homemade stuff.

Combine all ingredients in a large bowl. Beat or stir well. Pour into large crockery jug or bowl, or into your commercial yogurt-maker. Cover. Set in warm place (e.g. over hot air register, or in your warming oven; somewhere over warm, *not* hot, air.)

Let set till thick (6 to 10 hours, usually) *then* chill. Or add Jello, stir well to dissolve, let it set 30 minutes longer and then chill. This recipe makes 4 cups (1 lL).

At breakfast time, Lloyd the Bear is a predictable presence on the Lull Bay tide flats. He isn't a fast mover, but then you could speculate that under his black, furry hide lies the soul of an aesthete, slowly savoring the spirituality of each leaf, berry or blade he communes with, or eats! Then again, you might attribute Lloyd's phlegmatic expression and rather blubbery body shape to a sensitively shy nature; an introvert, contemplative philosopher of a bear at heart. Or maybe Lloyd's a secret conservationist, methodically plopping fertile bear-paddies on the acidic inlet soil.

I like Lloyd. I like his reliable black blob of a presence, unassumingly munching Lull Bay grass. Lloyd's an old pal. No demands. No complaints. One constant aspect of life in Knight Inlet.

He likes these hot cakes with maple syrup - mm,delicious! The Australian friend after whom he was named likes them with steak, eggs and Aussie beer!! But most guests like them best with smoked salmon pate (see recipe p. 85) and sour cream.

Lloyd The Bear's Buckwheat Pancakes

Serves 3 to 6 (makes 12)

1/2 cup	all-purpose flour	125 mL
1/2 cup	buckwheat flour	125 mL
1/2 tsp.	salt	2 mL
1 tsp.	baking soda	5 mL
	1 egg	
1 cup	buttermilk	250 mL
	or	
7/8 cup	milk and	225 mL
2 Tbsp.	lemon juice or vinegar	30 mL

Sift dry ingredients into medium bowl. Add egg, buttermilk and butter. Stir to blend. Add more milk if batter is too thick. Drop spoonfuls onto moderately hot griddle and fry both sides until done in the middle.

Variation:

Buckwheat-Banana Hotcakes

Thinly slice 1 1/2 bananas. Drop slices quickly onto and over uncooked tops of frying pancakes. Then turn when brown on bottom and fry with banana slices until done (test centers with a knife).

I named the next recipe for Aunt Molly. Not that Aunt Molly's a great cook. She'll admit that. But Molly's definitely an inspiration to our resort lifestyle. Molly is our "absentee auntie," meaning she's chosen to live on an isolated island in Greece. She's 64, independent, a loner; loves to write (historical articles); resembles Rex Harrison; is an inveterate walker of goat trails, rescuer of stray cats and people; avoider of cities, cars and modern conveniences; and defender of underdog causes. Mainly, Molly's the kindest person I know. She's "family."

So we named our first lodge *The Aunt Molly*. She symbolized a channel for our independence, a challenge to establish our own freedom and personality in this isolated inlet. Also, through the resort we could feel close to people, create, in a sense, a "fishing family." This being how Molly operates, her name seemed an apt symbol for our life and home here.

Molly never eats pancakes in Greece! She prefers the smoky, wood-fired breads at her village. When she visits us, though, she likes them as a change.

Aunt Molly's Apple or Banana Pancakes

Serves 6 to 8 (makes 12 to 14 medium pancakes)
Good with butter, syrup, maybe some sour cream.

1 cup	all-purpose flour	*250 mL*
1/4 cup	sugar	*65 mL*
2¼ tsp.	baking powder	*12 mL*
1/4 tsp.	cinnamon	*1 mL*
1/2 tsp.	salt	*2 mL*
2 Tbsp.	melted butter or margarine, reserve on warm surface	*30 mL*
	2 eggs	
1 cup	milk	*250 mL*
	1 tart apple, unpeeled grated	

Sift dry ingredients into a medium bowl. Set aside. Just before serving time, beat milk and eggs into sifted dry ingredients. Stir in melted butter. *Then* stir in grated apple. Heat largest frying pan (I use three cast-iron skillets at once) with bacon fat (unhealthy, but tastes great!) or butter, to cover bottoms well. Drop large spoonfuls batter into pans and fry until bubbly on top. Then turn and fry uncooked side. Serve immediately.

Variation:

For banana pancakes, omit apple. Slice one large banana thinly and drop slices on uncooked tops of pancakes in pan. Turn and fry until done through.

Ellen marched into the resort about three years ago, pulled out her sewing kit, set her jaw, and methodically proceeded to darn all our socks. Though 70 years old and seemingly frail, she was here with husband Eric to fish, and fish she determinedly did - 12 hours a day!

At dinner time, the old couple would boat back early for the "cocktail hour." Eric donned his tweedy jacket for the ritual and with savored ceremony, mixed them drinks at the bar. Then Ellen, in soft Arizona tones, would recount her favorite recipes.

Serve these crepe-like pancakes, for instance, as a breakfast-appetizer - two or three per person. They should be lightly browned and crispy on each side. Serve with syrup, your favorite jam, or maybe some sour cream.

Ellen's Swedish Pancakes

Serves 4 to 6 (makes 12 to 16 pancakes)

1 cup	all-purpose flour	*250 mL*
1/2 tsp.	salt	*2 mL*
	2 eggs	
1 cup	milk	*250 mL*
1/2 tsp.	fine-grated lemon rind	*2 mL*
1 Tbsp.	melted butter or margarine	*15 mL*

Sift dry ingredients together. Beat eggs and milk together in a small bowl. Add lemon rind and melted butter and add to flour mixture. Beat until smooth. Heat 6" iron skillet. Lightly brush with oil before cooking each pancake.

Pour 3 Tbsp. to 1/4 cup (about 70 mL) of the batter into hot skillet. Swirl quickly to cover bottom. Cook until lightly browned on bottom. Then flip and cook other side. Watch closely - it only takes a few seconds.

Fold each pancake in half and serve hot, immediately, or keep warm in oven while you cook remaining pancakes. Then serve all on platter.

Note: You may need to add more milk to batter after a while. It gets thicker as it stands.

I've never actually visited Boogie Bay. I know there's a logging camp there, and each morning a local "school boat" used to transport children to Minstrel Island.

"Boogie Bay" - sounds intriguing? I've purposely mis-spelled the name. The official version is Boughie, named during the original British exploration of the coast.

Boogie Bay Eggs Benedict

Serves 4 to 8

For this breakfast-brunch dish, use Aunt Dot's Biscuits (recipe page 60) and a variety of creamy spreads: either smoked salmon pate, or cream cheese and chives, or guacamole. I make everything ahead, then simply poach the eggs to serve.

Early in the morning, or night before, make one or more of the following spreads:

Chive-Cheese Spread

8 oz.	plain cream cheese	*250 mL*

Soften cheese and whip. Add chopped green onions or chives to taste. Chill.

Smoked Salmon Pate

See recipe p.*85*

Guacamole

See recipe under Crab Chalupas, p.96

Next make:

Hollandaise Sauce

(I make it 1 to 3 hours ahead, chill, then bring it to room temperature 1 hour before serving.)

3/4 cup	butter, softened	*200 mL*
2½ tsp.	fresh lemon juice	*12 mL*
	3 egg yolks	
	dash 'fines herbes' (optional)	
	dash cayenne	
1-3 tsp.	finely chopped green onion	*10-15 mL*

In double-boiler top, combine and whip with hand whisk 1/4 cup (75 mL) of the butter, lemon juice, egg yolks and seasonings. Whip till foamy, then add 1/4 cup (75 mL) more of the remaining butter, cut in pieces. Whisk until it begins to thicken, then add the remaining 1/4 cup (75 mL) of butter and whisk until thick as mayonnaise. Immediately remove boiler top from hot water and add green onion.

To Serve: Split biscuits and spread halves thickly with any one, or combinations of, the spreads (e.g. cream cheese plus guacamole, or the salmon pate is good with thin slices of avocado arranged over it on biscuit halves.)

Poach eggs to just cooked. Place one egg on each biscuit-half, or over two biscuit-halves (depending on number of people to serve), or between two biscuit-halves, like a sandwich. Pour hollandaise over. Serve quickly!

Tyee are huge salmon, weighing thirty pounds or more. Catching a Tyee is the dream of every guest. Tyee usually fight — sneakily, long and hard. He who brings one in deserves and needs this huge omelet.

The Tyee Omelet

(Crab, Smoked Salmon or Sausage Omelet)

Serves one large appetite or make one omelet and cut it in half for two people.

Great filler during boating or camping trips.

First, prepare optional fillings:

1-2 Tbsp.	smoked salmon, chopped	15-30 mL
	or	
2 Tbsp.-1/4 cup	Polish Sausage or salami, chopped	30-50 mL
1/4-1/2 cup	or drained fresh crab	50-100 mL
1/3-1/2 cup	old sharp cheddar, grated	50-100 mL
	2 large eggs	
	handful chopped parsley and green onion, mixed	
1/4 cup	skim milk powder	75 mL
1-2 Tbsp.	water	15-30 mL
1/4 tsp.	salt	1 mL
	dash pepper	
	liberal dash 'fines herbes' (a commercial herb blend)	

For crab omelet add:
        pinch dried leaf tarragon

Beat all ingredients (except cheese) well with fork.
Heat small 8 inch skillet over high heat.
Add whichever filling you choose to beaten egg mixture in bowl, stir, pour into hot skillet, turn heat to low, tilt pan to distribute egg evenly. Sprinkle cheese over, and cover. Cook until it begins to "jell." Lift edges of omelet to allow top liquid to run under (tilt pan). Check bottom occasionally to see how brown it's getting. Cook, covered, until bottom is golden brown and set but still slightly creamy on top. Fold over and serve.

26

Mornings in the resort begin with early darkness, hot coffee and homemade bread smells. Line-ups for the bathroom; long underwear against the dank chill. By sunrise, red boats sputter out to the kelp bed areas around Hoeya Head.

This souffle makes a great beginning - or a fine welcome home - for the fishermen.

Hoeya Cheese Souffle

Serves 4

This souffle is excellent for breakfast, lunch or dinner. Never lets you down; always rises with crisp brown crust on top and bottom. Easy to make, too, since souffle can mostly be prepared ahead. No last minute flurry!

	4 eggs	
3 Tbsp.	melted margarine or butter	45 mL
1 cup	milk	250 mL
1/4 cup	all-purpose flour	60 mL
1/2 tsp.	salt	2 mL
	dash cayenne	
1 tsp.	*Coleman's* dried mustard powder	5 mL
1/2 tsp.	dried leaf marjoram	2 mL
1/8 tsp.	'fines herbes' blend (commercial herb mix, I use *Spice Islands)*	1 mL
1 cup	old sharp cheddar cheese, - coarsely grated	250 mL
	2-4 slices crisp fried bacon, chopped (or pinch of commercial dried bacon bits or handful smoked salmon, chopped)	
2 Tbsp.		30-50 mL
1/4 cup	chopped chives and parsley mixed	

Separate eggs, placing whites in large bowl, yolks in medium bowl. Heat milk (do *not* allow it to boil). In double boiler, melt margarine and gradually stir in flour. Slowly stir in the hot milk and seasonings. Cook and stir until smooth and very thick. Add cheese and stir until completely melted, then add bacon (or smoked salmon), chives and parsley. With spatula, stir yolks until blended. Slowly stir the hot cheese sauce into yolks. When yolks and sauce completely blended, set aside to cool.

Beat reserved egg whites stiff, and fold gradually into cooled cheese sauce, a bit at first, then all the whites. Pour into ungreased 1½ quart casserole. With spoon, make or scoop shallow "well" 1 inch (3 cm) from edge of souffle. Later this will puff into a "crown" in oven. Bake, uncovered, 1 hour at 300° F.

Serve immediately! Dig to bottom for that crust. Quite filling!

It's a silent, mock drama out there. "Red boats" versus our competitor's "green." Both camps warily count each other's fish, explode into sneak water fights, occasionally raid each other's crab traps; constantly lie over fish catches.

Behind all the competitive joking, both camps like, depend on and help each other in many small, invisible ways. Red boats vs. green is, in fact, a comic "front."

Crab Quiche

Serves 4 to 8 for brunch, lunch or dinner
Makes one 9-inch pie

Make Aunt Dot's Butter Pastry (recipe page 132) or use half of Audrey's Lard Pastry (recipe page 132), roll out and fit into 9-inch pie plate.

1 cup	sliced mushrooms	250 mL
2 Tbsp.	brandy	30 mL
1 cup	grated Swiss or cheddar cheese	250 mL
1 cup	drained, flaked crabmeat - fresh or canned - chilled	250 mL
1 cup	evaporated milk, or cream	250 mL
	3 eggs	
1/8 tsp. scant	nutmeg	1 mL
1/8 tsp.	dried leaf tarragon	1 mL
1 tsp.	salt	5 mL
1 Tbsp.	all-purpose flour	15 mL
	handful chives or green onions, and parsley.	

Chop finely, a handful of fresh chives and some parsley. Slice mushrooms thinly and marinate five minutes in brandy. Drain. In medium bowl, beat together milk, eggs and seasonings. Add chives and parsley.

Layer the drained mushrooms, crab and cheese in the crust. Stir liquid mixture well and pour into shell. Spread chives and parsley evenly around if they tend to lump up. Bake at 375° for 40 minutes or until set and golden brown, but middle still wobbles slightly. Cool on rack 5 to 10 minutes. Serve in wedges.

Ruth's Eggplant Mellanzane

Serves 4 to 6

Picture an eggplant and cheese pie, or eggplant pizza. That's how mellanzane looks. Tastes like Eggplant Parmesan and is, in fact, an easy variation of that. Created by a Swiss draftslady, gourmet, friend, Ruth.

2 Tbsp.	margarine or olive oil	30 mL
	1 large onion - chopped	
	4 cloves garlic - crushed	
	lots chopped parsley (1/2 cup or so)	
5½ oz.	can tomato paste	156 mL
19 oz.	can whole undrained tomatoes	540 mL
1/4 cup	dry red wine	75 mL
2 tsp.	dried leaf basil	10 mL
2 tsp.	dried leaf oregano	10 mL
	salt to taste (1 tsp. or more)	
	liberal dash cayenne - to taste	
	2 large eggplants	
or	1 large eggplant	
	plus 1 or 2 zucchini or more	
1/2 lb.	medium or mild cheddar	250 mL
	or	
	Monterey Jack cheese, grated.	

Heat margarine in heavy saucepan and saute onion, parsley and garlic until soft. Add remaining ingredients (except eggplant and cheese). Simmer, covered, 30 minutes to 1 hour. Stir occasionally, uncover, simmer until very thick (30 to 45 minutes or more), stirring occasionally. Meanwhile, slice eggplants thinly. Don't peel unless skin tastes bitter. If using zucchini, steam to tender-crisp in quarter-inch slices.

Arrange eggplant slices on pan. Brush each slice with olive oil. Broil until slices are spotted-brown. Turn. Brush uncooked sides with olive oil and broil until tender. Reserve.

When tomato sauce is *very* thick, remove from heat. Butter 9" pie plate. Spread with a thin amount of sauce to cover the bottom. Reserve one-quarter of the sauce for top. Arrange a layer of eggplant (and optional zucchini) over sauce. Spread some tomato sauce over each eggplant slice and sprinkle some cheese over all. Repeat layers until all vegetables are in "pie," ending with top layer of tomato sauce and final 1/2 cup (125 mL) cheese.

Bake 400° F., 20 minutes or until hot and bubbling. Let "sit" 5 minutes. Serve in wedges.

Soups

One cold, January day at Minstrel Island our small lodge, *The Aunt Molly,* burned. When fire broke out, we were leisurely working at a nearby float, hammering down floorboards for a new, larger lodge. We hoped to complete the lodge in a year — ready for the *next* fishing season.

It was a horrifying day. We watched flames gut the interior of our home as swiftly as you'd gut a salmon. With some sense of irony, I pictured my latest Crepes Suzette experiment sizzling alongside my clothes and recipes.

Luckily most of the area's community had dropped by for beer. So with much struggle, we saved *The Aunt Molly's* outer shell and our fishing equipment.

Off the community moved us, by boat and by foot, to a nearby summer cottage. And that night we held a wake. We farewelled *The Aunt Molly:* our past sweat, labor and love for her. It was a helluva celebration!

Next morning we plotted for the future: the *full-pressure* building of the new lodge, as quickly as possible! We'd pour our energy into that and sell what was left of *The Aunt Molly*. Trouble was, we had only three months to do it in before our fishing season opened.

So began my first taste of community protection. I, who had always been cautiously independent, suddenly found the Minstrel area people uniting to help us out. Here they came daily, boating in from Cracroft and Bones Bay and Minstrel itself to work eight hours a day on our lodge. Generously, wives cooked pot-luck meals so everyone could get together up at the Swallow Inn. For three days my gutsy neighbor Marilyn, from Bones Bay, uncomplainingly labored over our massive smoke-damaged laundry. I felt bewildered, embarrassed, overwhelmed and choked-up by the quality of caring.

After a solid week of heavy hammering, busy measuring, whine of skill saws, our dream lodge sported walls, windows, even a roof. We couldn't believe it. So quick. Now we could manage the building ourselves. Area people returned to their own jobs and lives. They felt like good friends.

That winter I took on simple carpentry jobs, and felt proud of my contribution. Although I was a klutz with measuring, I got pretty good at cutting 45° angles with the skill saw. Somehow I still continued experimenting with cookery: lots of hot soups, hot chile dishes, and ..... baked Alaskas!

I will never forget Minstrel area's people: their care, assistance and protection. With them, we rebuilt our lives and our new resort, *Sailcone*.

And whenever I make a hot soup I think back to those cold winter days when steaming bowls helped to thaw the chilled fingers of those who had come to help.

In this often cold, stormy climate, heat is life-sustaining. Hot, filling soups, hot whiskeys, steaming coffees; true comforters to chilled people.

I declare "meditative hibernation." During gray coast days, I bury myself beneath piles of blankets and triple sweaters, my feet and hot water bottle inseparable. Just taking time to think, and write, and drift ... inwards.

When sunny weather breaks through, I surface, feeling as transparent as the light. Time to direct my energy.

Magnetized, I waltz sun-warmed around the lodge: kneading

breads in kitchen-bright pools; sunning outside in hot green-ocean light.

Evenings flow in soft gold waves up inlet mountains. I research and read recipes, sipping hot chocolate with warm people.

Fresh "Mintpea" Soup

Serves 8

A light, easy puree of frozen peas, leaf mint and chicken stock. I like this soup as a first course with dinner. Goes well with seafood dishes and a cornbread or salad, or with seafood (e.g. jambalaya) and a simple vegetable. Serve 1/2 cup (125 mL) soup to each person, as a first course, or increase each serving for a soup lunch.

2 cups	chicken stock	500 mL
	dried leaf tarragon,	
	"fines herbes" or "Bouquet Garni"	
1½ lb.	frozen peas	750 g
	1 medium onion, sliced thin	
	1 small carrot, sliced thin	
	2 torn lettuce leaves	
	3-4 fresh mint leaves	
	or	
1/2-1 tsp.		
or more	dried leaf mint, to taste, (keep it subtly mint, though!)	3-5 mL
1 tsp.	sugar	5 mL
3 Tbsp.	butter	45 mL
1 cup	heavy cream or evaporated milk (I use the milk)	250 mL
2 tsp.	salt	10 mL
	pepper to taste	
	croutons or chopped green onions for garnish	

To chicken stock add liberal dash tarragon and fines herbes. Then add vegetables, mint and sugar and simmer until tender. Discard mint leaves. Puree all, gradually, in a blender. Pour puree batches into saucepan. Add butter, milk, salt and pepper and stir to melt butter. *Don't* let boil or it curdles! Garnish each bowl with croutons or chopped green onions.

As long as I've known him, Will's been free. He's had careers, and worked hard at them: logger, musician, fisherman, artist, farmer, chef, furniture maker, mechanic. Too adventuresome to stop. Maybe that's why Will seems so youthful. He's a big guy; dark, rosy-cheeked, perpetually puffs an aromatic pipe. He emanates cheerful, strong energy. His carving of woods and artistry with iron indicate an eye sensitive to beauty of form; delicacy of line. Somehow, Will brings to life the character, texture and glow of his material. Our golden alder table was carved by Will.

One day in his Freshwater Bay cabin, Will served me this buttery soup, passed on from his Russian Mama.

Will's Roosian Borscht

Serves 8 to 16
Prepare early in the day and leave to "marinate." Cut down on butter if you wish although this will weaken the rich flavor.

	4 large potatoes	
	2-3 large scrubbed beets	
	2 medium onions	
1/2 -		
3/4 lb.	butter	250-400 g
	1 medium cabbage	
8 cups	water	2 L
	2 chopped green peppers	
19 oz.	can tomatoes, undrained	540 mL
	salt and cayenne to taste	
	lots dried dillweed to taste	

Dice and set aside the beets and potatoes. Finely chop onions and saute in lots of butter (1/4 lb.) to brown well. Set aside. Add 1/2 lb (250 g) butter and finely chopped cabbage to pan and saute until soft.

In a large pot, bring water to boil, add beets and potatoes and cook until just tender. Then add all other vegetables and seasonings and simmer until everything is tender. Remove from heat and let sit until serving time.

To serve: Reheat soup, ladle into deep bowls, garnish each with a large blob of sour cream and a sprinkle of dillweed over.

We dig our best clams in the narrow channel near Minstrel Island named, mysteriously, "The Blowhole." Maybe because the westerly roars through that passage like a pressure gauge.

"The Blowhole" Clam Chowder

Serves 6 to 8

Make early in day so herbs have time to "grip" this thick, creamy soup. Good with Sennebec Hill bread (recipe page 74) or cornmeal molasses bread (recipe page 71).

1/2 lb.	bacon	*250 g*
2 cups	2 or 3 potatoes - to make cubes	*500 mL*
	1 large onion, finely chopped	
4 cups	chopped clam meat	
	or	
2 29 oz.	cans baby clams if you have no fresh clams	*2x 1L*
2 cups	clam juice (add water if necessary)	*500 mL*
1/4 cup	all-purpose flour	*75 mL*
3/4 tsp.	dried leaf 'Bouquet Garni' (commercial herb blend)	*3 mL*
3/4 tsp.	dried powdered thyme	*3 mL*
1 tsp.	salt	*5 mL*
1/2 tsp	white pepper	*2 mL*
2 cups	milk (I use milk powder plus leftover clam juice)	*500 mL*
2 cups	evaporated milk or cream	*500 mL*
2 Tbsp.	butter	*30 mL*

Dice bacon and brown in large heavy pot. Add potatoes and cook 3-4 minutes, stirring occasionally. Add onions and continue cooking over low heat until vegetables are soft but not brown. Stir in flour, 2 cups (500 mL) of clam juice and seasonings. Bring to boil. Add clams and simmer 10 minutes. Then add milk, cream and butter, and stir until melted. Don't boil or it curdles.

Irene and Dan are traveling fishery officers. Middle-aged and energetic, they live on their homey boat, connecting us all with messages and news. They're wanderers, exploring the coast through their work.

Whenever Dan and Irene boat up to take a fish count or check the salmon runs, I'll rush to finish my chores. Out comes the cookie bowl and the teapot, and our favorite topic - food!

Irene's Fish Mulligan

Serves 6 to 12
Best made early in the day, or 2 to 3 hours before serving.

2 lb.	fish fillets	1 kg
	or	
1 lb.	canned salmon (or more to taste)	500 g
	4 medium carrots, diced	
1 cup	celery, chopped	250 mL
	4 medium potatoes, chopped	
	2 medium onions, sliced	
4 cups	at least - water, to cover	1 L
1½ tsp.	mixed whole pickling spices (a blend)	7 mL
	1 bay leaf	
	salt and pepper to taste	
1/2 cup	cream or evaporated milk	125 mL
	(I prefer milk)	

To make the stock, combine all ingredients except fish and cream in a heavy saucepan and cook, covered, until tender-crisp. Skin the fish fillets and cut into large chunks. Saute lots of butter until partially cooked and flaking (don't try to saute the canned salmon, though). When vegetables are cooked, set pot to one side and add fish. (Chill at this point if made ahead, then re-heat at serving time.). Add a little butter to taste if desired. Stir in cream and serve garnished with parsley.

When *The Aunt Molly* burned down we lived for a while in an abandoned summer cottage. It was called "The Lighthouse" and had once been a restaurant run by two sweet old ladies famed for their home-baked doughnuts. I subsequently decided The Lighthouse contained a resident ghost: George, I christened him.

George loved to drop lightbulbs on my head, but otherwise he was harmless. I suspect he may even have enjoyed my cooking creations, so I named a recipe after him.

George's Tarragon-Tomato Soup

Serves 4 as a first course
Appeals to guests who like easy recipes for entertaining. A light, fresh, herb and wine soup. Make it early in the day or 1 hour before serving. Time allows the tarragon to blend in. Can double or triple recipe.

1/4 cup	butter	75 g
1-1/3 cups	chopped onion	300 mL
	6 whole tomatoes	
l/2 cup	dry white wine	125 mL
1 Tbsp.	sugar	15 mL
1 tsp.	dried leaf tarragon	5 mL
	salt and pepper to taste	
	sour cream and chives for garnish	

In large saucepan with lid, melt butter and saute onion until golden. Meanwhile, drop tomatoes in boiling water and boil until skins begin to split. Pour cold water over tomatoes, peel off and discard skins. Chop tomatoes and add to cooked onions. Add wine, sugar and tarragon. Cut a circle of wax paper the size of the saucepan, butter it and place it directly on top of the soup. This will prevent skim from collecting on the surface. Simmer, covered, over low heat 45 minutes.

Cool 10 minutes. Puree soup in blender, then sieve or strain into saucepan. Add salt and pepper to taste. Set to one side or chill.

To Serve: Heat soup, pour into bowls. Garnish each bowl with spoonful of sour cream and sprinkle of chopped chives or scallions.

37

We often hold "mussel hunts." Guests from all parts of North America flail through slimy weed, gathering mussels for dinner. Although I hate to scrub mussels, people eagerly help out, and we all enjoy the end result.

Mussels should be gathered, de-bearded and scrubbed early in the morning or day before. Change their water (I use ocean) every two or four hours before your meal.

Mussel Bouillabaisse

Serves 4 as a main dish, or 8 as a first course

A cross between a chowder and stew, this is a very simple recipe. Good with French bread, or corn loaf (recipe page 75). The hardest part is gathering the mussels. However, I notice that fish markets now sell them fresh at low prices.

Early in morning, gather and clean 8 to 12 cups largest mussels (80 to 90 mussels, or 3 quarts or Litres). Cover with water until serving time.

Prepare basic sauce:

1/4 cup	olive oil	75 mL
2/3 cup	minced onion (I use Cuisinart here)	150 mL
1/3 cup	minced canned pimento	100 mL
	3 garlic cloves - crushed	150 mL
7½ oz.	can tomato *sauce* (not the paste)	205 mL
2 tsp.	salt	10 mL
	1 tomato - peeled, seeded, chopped	
1/3 cup	dry white wine	100 mL
2 tsp.	dried leaf basil	10 mL
2 tsp.	dried leaf oregano	10 mL

In heavy saucepan, heat oil, saute onion, pimento and garlic. Stir in rest of ingredients except mussels. Simmer 30 min. until thick (may take longer), and transfer to broad-bottomed pot.

To Serve: 10 minutes before serving, drain mussels well. Heat sauce. Chop parsley to garnish. Boil mussels in sauce, covered, 3 to 5 minutes, just until they half-open. Stir occasionally. With slotted spoon, lift mussels to soup bowls, and divide sauce among bowls, pouring evenly over the mussels. Garnish each serving with parsley.

Salads

In the resort, as on the coast, life is often complex: a struggle to gain time for self and for enjoyment of people vs. the hard work of existence here. Our harsh protagonist is the land: stormy climate, cold winds and rains, isolating distances.

I use my sense of humor and my imagination to attack my resort "maintenance routine." While scrubbing the outhouse, I paste new jokes on the door; I salute amorous spiders on the ceiling or starfish creeping below. As I crank the generator, I picture myself floating in moons of translucent jellyfish, suspended, absorbing salty winds, Lloyd Bear rooting the mudflats, guests shuffling cards.

I'm a warrior! Staving off molds from my vegetables, sharing tribulations with our guides - my pals, heroically vacuuming the lodge. My apron banner vanquishes dirt and people-confusion. Will the cookie bowl survive today's seige?

One hour of each day, though, I claim a time of peace. To sink into wharf-warmth, rocked by Lull Bay. Or to read - alone.

Renewed, soothed, I rejoin the lodge. Curious to explore our guests, and cooking. Or salads. Especially salads!

Salads provoke me to more complexity; a leafy world of herb-green crunchiness. Deepening tastes; unified through the unique dressing of my day's mood.

Nine years ago, we couldn't afford to fly fresh vegetables to the resort. I served cabbage.... endlessly. *All* my salads were cabbage. In desperation I began to experiment with different nut, fruit and dressing combinations. This salad was my first proud invention.

40

The Hoeya Head Slaw

Serves 6 to 8

Make salad and dressing early in day. Chill.

Dressing:

1 cup	vegetable oil (preferably safflower)	250 mL
3/4 cup	cider vinegar	200 mL
1/2 cup	brown sugar	125 mL
1/2 tsp.	dried leaf tarragon	2 mL
1 tsp.	salt	5 mL
1 tsp.	*Coleman's* dry mustard powder	5 mL
1/2 tsp.	dried leaf marjoram	2 mL
	(or oregano or mint)	
1/2 tsp.	garlic powder	2 mL
1/4 tsp.	dried dillweed	1 mL

Combine in large jar with lid. Shake well. Chill until one hour before serving time, then bring to room temperature.

Salad

1-2 cups	raw, shelled peanuts	250-500 mL
1/4 cup	raw sesame seeds	75 mL
1/4 cup	poppy seeds	75 mL
1/2 cup	raw sunflower seeds	125 mL
	1-1½ bananas - sliced in thick chunks	
	1-1½ tart apples - chopped into large pieces	
	2 carrots - coarsely grated	
	1 green pepper - chopped	
	2 celery stalks and heads - diced	
	3 green onions - chopped	
1/2 lb.	broccoli - the florets peeled and sliced	250 g
	1 medium head cabbage, shredded	
	handful chopped parsley	
1-2 cups	seeded muscat raisins	250-500 mL

Roast nuts and seeds in separate pans, at 350° F. until done. Cool. Reserve for garnish.

Chop apple and slice bananas thickly. Cover with prepared vegetables, and sprinkle with raisins. Cover. Chill in fridge until serving time.

To Serve: Shake dressing. Pour all over salad. Toss thoroughly. Sprinkle all seeds and nuts over. Toss again. Serve.

Note: This salad is also great with minted cooked peas, and/or sliced olives (black or green) or sliced cauliflower.

41

Blue Cheese, Walnut and Pineapple Slaw

Serves 6 to 8

Sweet, salty, nutty and crunchy!

This salad was inspired by two guests from Yakima, Washington: Glen Cornelius and John Stammerjohan.

John Stammerjohan's Garlicky Blue Cheese Dressing

Makes 3 to 4 cups (about 1 L)

Excellent dressing for any coleslaws, also a great dip for vegetable crudites. Make at least 2 hours ahead so flavors have time to "meld."

6 oz.	(1¼ cup) blue cheese	225 g
8 oz.	softened plain cream cheese	250 g
1/2 cup	milk (I use evaporated tinned milk plus water)	125 mL
1 Tbsp. or more	juice of 1/2 lemon - to taste	15 mL
2 cups	commercial mayonnaise or salad dressing 2 large garlic cloves - crush into above mix	500 mL
1 tsp.	salt	5 mL
1/2 tsp.	pepper	2 mL

Combine ingredients in medium bowl. Beat all, using lowest speed of mixer. Should be lumpy (so don't use your blender - it makes dressing too smooth!). Chill, covered, in jar.

Salad:

1 cup	walnut halves or pieces	250 mL
	1 or 2 handfuls poppy seeds	
	1-2 tart green apples, chopped into large chunks	
	1/2 bunch parsley	
	3 or 4 green onions (or more)	
1/2-1 lb.	broccoli, peeled and finely sliced	250-500 g
19 oz.	can pineapple chunks, drained	540 mL
	1-1½ medium heads cabbage, shredded	
2/3-1 cup	currants	200-250 mL

Toast walnuts and poppy seeds. Reserve for final garnish. Chop apple into large bowl. Cover with chopped parsley, onions, pineapple and broccoli, and lastly cabbage. Sprinkle currants over all.

To Serve: Toss in only enough dressing to coat the cabbage. Taste to check, add more if you like. Toss in walnuts. Sprinkle over poppy seeds. Serve.

Beet And Olive Slaw

Serves 6
An interesting combination of tastes. A filling salad.

Cooked Horseradish Dressing

Makes 1½ cups (350 mL).   Make early in day.

2 Tbsp.	brown sugar	30 mL
2 Tbsp.	honey	30 mL
2 Tbsp.	flour	30 mL
1½ tsp.	Coleman's dry mustard powder	7 mL
1 tsp.	salt	5 mL
	1 well-beaten egg	
1 cup	milk	250 mL
1/4 cup	cider vinegar	75 mL
2 Tbsp.	butter or margarine	30 mL
1/2 tsp.	powdered ginger	2 mL
1-2 Tbsp.	prepared commercial horseradish	20-30 mL
1/2 cup	safflower oil	125 mL

In top of double boiler, stir together brown sugar, honey, flour, mustard and salt. Add egg and stir to make a paste. Stir in milk, slowly add vinegar and cook over hot water until thick, stirring consistently. Add butter, ginger and horseradish, stir well. Pour into large jar and chill. When cool, pour dressing into blender or Cuisinart and blend in oil until smooth. Return dressing to fridge and chill until one hour before serving. Then bring to room temperature.

Salad

1/2-1 cup	walnut pieces	125-250 mL
	poppy seeds to taste	
	4 green onions	
	1/2 bunch parsley	
14 oz.	can sliced beets	398 mL
7 oz.	(1/2 can) pitted black olives	200 mL
	1 medium head of cabbage	

Toast walnuts and poppy seeds. Reserve for garnish. Chop onions and parsley into large salad bowl. Add halved beet slices and halved olives. Cover all with finely shredded cabbage (do not use a Cuisinart - it bruises the cabbage and makes the salad watery). Chill.

To Serve: Add walnuts to salad. Pour dressing over all. Toss well. Garnish with toasted poppy seeds.

We named our second resort *Sailcone* - after the high land-hump on Hoeya Head. It's a mountain of contrasts. A solid vitality imprisoned behind furry trees and rock. During my cooking day I often simply stop - and watch - Sail Cone. Poised, mass energy crouches. Sail Cone and surrounding mountains contain their own paradoxical life: a delicate upward soaring; an earthbound stolidity. Mutely, they resist ocean tumult. Rock spires raise subtle exaltation to the winds.

Sailcone's Caesar
Serves 6 to 8

I love Caesar Salad - as much a prince among salads as Sail Cone is among the mountains of Knight Inlet.

Dressing

	3 cloves garlic - crushed	
1/4 cup	safflower oil	75 mL
	1 egg yolk	
1 Tbsp.	lemon juice (fresh)	15 mL
1 Tbsp.	red wine vinegar	15 mL
1 Tbsp.	Worcestershire sauce	15 mL
	1-2 anchovy fillets - finely chopped	
1/2 tsp.	salt	2 mL

Shake well until cloudy. Set aside in fridge (shake occasionally). Bring to room temperature before serving.

Salad

	8 slices bacon	
1/4-1/2 cup	Parmesan (preferably not commercially packaged product, best quality is in local meat markets, cheese shops, or Greek/Italian markets.)	75-125 mL
1 cup	herbed or cheese croutons	250 mL
	2 medium heads romaine or 1 huge head	
	2-3 green onions - chopped	
optional	12-16 cherry tomatoes	

Fry bacon until crisp, drain on paper towel and crumble. Set aside in fridge. Grate Parmesan and reserve. Prepare croutons and reserve.

Tear lettuce into bite-size pieces, wash, drain and pat gently dry. Place in large salad bowl, add onions, cover bowl and chill. Halve tomatoes. Place in covered container. Chill.

To Serve: Shake dressing well. Pour over salad and toss well. Toss in Parmesan. Toss. Add more Parmesan (to 1/2 cup - 125 mL) if too bland. Over salad sprinkle the optional tomatoes and croutons and bacon. Serve immediately.

"Jude" (or Judy) is partner and wife to "John the Cook " (pg. 84) down at our neighboring "green boats" camp. She's also my closest female pal in the inlet. A gruff, honest Australian, big hearted; courageous in obvious, and unexpected, ways. Judy has biked across Australia, worked prawn boats and cattle ranches, and she dares to be sensitive. Behind her direct blue eyes hides an artist's soul, delicately responsive to nature and to her own inner expression. In the inlet, Judy allows herself to paint. And one day I glimpsed a snow maiden she had sculpted. The graceful flowing lines and fragile shy beauty revealed... Judy.

Like me, Judy enjoys fresh salads. For her, this recipe:

Jude's Artichoke Green

Serves 4 to 6

The salad uses a creamy, tarragon and anchovy dressing -subtle background to the tang of artichokes.

Dressing

1/2 cup	tarragon wine vinegar	125 mL
	1 egg	
1/2 tsp.	dried leaf tarragon	2 mL
	1 clove garlic	
2 tsp.	anchovy paste	10 mL
	or 2 anchovy fillets	
1 tsp.	salt	5 mL
1 cup	safflower oil	250 mL
1/2 cup	dairy sour cream	125 mL
2 Tbsp.	chopped chives	30 mL
1/4 cup	chopped parsley	75 mL

Blend in blender or Cuisinart the vinegar, egg, garlic, anchovy paste, salt and tarragon. Slowly drizzle in oil, blend until thick and creamy, then add remaining ingredients.
Chill in covered container.

Salad

	2 scallions (green onions) or more	
	large handful parsley	
1-2 cups	fresh mushrooms	250-500 mL
14 oz.	1/2 to 1 can	398 mL
	artichoke hearts, well-drained	

                handful alfalfa sprouts (optional)
                1 large head romaine lettuce or
                1/2 head romaine and 1/2 head
                iceberg lettuce.
1 Tbsp.   capers, drained   15 mL
                toasted cashews
                    or
                Sesame seeds

Tear and wash lettuce. Pat dry in towel, set to one side. Slice scallions and mushrooms into large salad bowl, add parsley, artichoke hearts and sprouts. Cover with lettuce and sprinkle capers over all. Cover and chill.

To Serve: Shake dressing. Toss in just enough to coat the lettuce. Reserve remainder for other salads. Garnish with liberal sprinkle of raw cashews or toasted sesame seeds. Serve immediately.

Spencer's only a crow - just one of "the boys," hit-man for the flock.

Spencer's job is scoping out the wharf for fish guts. Being the most audacious member of the "gang," he's the guy right up front by the cleaning table, watching beadily for scraps. Spencer sneaks them back to the boys hiding in the trees. I'd swear that crow perpetually grins. He caws sarcasms from the roof, he cynically craps on the swallow nests, he mocks our task-oriented, wharfbound, work energy. Spencer's just having fun, playing spy vs. spy. He's the go-between, free to mock our seriousness. Spencer plagues us, angers us, adroitly frees us to laugh.

Spencer's Simple Romaine

Herb Dressing

Make early in day and chill. Bring to room temperature before serving.

1/2 cup	vegetable oil (preferably safflower)	125 mL
1/4 cup	red wine vinegar with garlic	75 mL
	1 to 2 garlic cloves - crushed	
1/3-1/2		
tsp.	salt	1-2 mL
1/2 tsp.	dry mustard powder	2 mL
3/4-1 tsp.	dried leaf basil or oregano or marjoram	3-5 mL
	or thyme or 'fines herbes' blend	
	liberal pinch fennel seeds - an optional	
	but tasty addition	

Optional - Use 1/2 tsp. any of the above herbs plus 1/4 tsp. any of the other herbs listed (2 mL & 1 mL), OR use 1/4 tsp. (1 mL) of any two of the above. You may add 1 bay leaf too. Combine in jar with lid and shake well.

Tarragon Dressing

Use 1/2 tsp. (2 mL) dried leaf tarragon and substitute 1/4 cup (75 mL) tarragon-wine vinegar for the garlic vinegar. Bring to room temperature before serving.

Salad

2 avocados - sliced
4-6 slices bacon, optional
sesame or poppy or sunflower seeds
2 chopped scallions
chopped parsley (I use lots)
(optional) chunks of white cheese
(optional) slices cauliflower or broccoli
1 large head romaine lettuce - tear,
     wash, pat dry.
8-12 cherry tomatoes

Fry bacon, drain, crumble and chill. Toast sesame seeds and reserve for garnish. Tear and wash lettuce, pat dry in towel. Combine scallions, parsley, cheese and avocado in large salad bowl. Cover with lettuce and chill until serving time. Halve tomatoes, place in covered container. Chill.

To Serve: Pour over salad just enough dressing to coat lettuce well, but not sog it. Toss. Garnish with tomatoes, bacon, seeds. Serve.

Every week, I radio-telephone my tedious grocery order to our city market. There's no privacy on the radio phone. We all hear all. We bore each other and sympathize with each other's lives. Everyone's visible.

I picture a communication web to every boat and home isolated on the coast. In fact, the radio phone *is* coast soap opera: a familiar drama of emergency calls and loving messages to families; of mundane conversations among fishermen to pass loneliness; of accident and weather reports - upon which we gauge our day's ocean activity; of my particular panic at voicing myself over the web.

But when the boxes of groceries finally arrive and dinner gets a lift from the fresh goods, I can relax again. This is when I indulge in something especially delicious....

Curried Avocado/Romaine Salad

Serves 6 to 8

A bacony, nut-tasting salad. Save up all your leftover bacon fat for this recipe.

Dressing

1/3 cup	safflower oil	100 mL
1/3 cup	melted bacon fat	100 mL
1/4 cup	red wine vinegar with garlic	75 mL
2 Tbsp.	dry white wine	30 mL
	2 cloves garlic - crushed	
2 tsp.	soy sauce (I use *Kikkoman* brand)	10 mL
1 tsp.	sugar	5 mL
1 tsp.	dry mustard powder	5 mL
1/2 tsp.	curry powder	2 mL
3/4 tsp.	salt	4 mL
1/4-1/2 tsp.	seasoned pepper	1-2 mL

Combine all ingredients in jar with lid. Shake well. Chill. Before serving time, warm up slightly to melt the bacon fat. Set to one side at room temperature.

Salad

1/2 cup	cashew nuts	*125 mL*
2-3 Tbsp.	sesame seeds	*30-45 mL*
	4-6 slices bacon, optional	
	or sliver slices of ham or any smoked meat	
	1 large head romaine or 2 bunches spinach, or combination of the two.	
	1 to 2 ripe avocados - peeled and sliced thick	
	half a tart apple - chopped	
14 oz.	one can artichoke hearts - drained, cut each in half	*398 mL*
	(optional) sweet onion rings or chopped green onions	

Toast nuts and seeds. Reserve for garnish. Fry bacon, drain, crumble and chill.

Tear lettuce into bite-size pieces, wash and pat dry with towel. Chop remaining ingredients into large salad bowl, arrange dried lettuce/spinach over all. Cover and chill.

To Serve: Pour over lettuce just enough dressing to moisten, but not enough to sog it (usually add it slowly). Toss, taste, add more if not piquant enough. Toss in cashews and sesame. Serve.

I use my cheapie lettuce - dryer for all salad concoctions. It dries vegetables superbly, but looks terrible--like a plastic tub. Sounds like a giant carnivorous moth as you whir the veggies around inside it. Not too popular during 6 a.m. coffee! - which is when I often like to make my dinner salad. Although our guests politely think I'm crazy, I find that making a salad early in the day, and using this "machine " gives a crispier fresher texture to the greens that emerge at dinner.

Spinach or Romaine with Mushrooms

Serves 4 to 6

Make garlic dressing early in day. Needs time to "marinate." Make salad up to one hour before serving. Chill.

Garlic Dressing

1/2 cup	safflower oil	125 mL
1/4 cup	white or wine vinegar	75 mL
	3 large cloves garlic - crushed	
1/4 tsp.	dried powdered thyme	1 mL
	1 large bay leaf	
1/2 tsp.	salt (to your taste)	2 mL

Mix ingredients in jar with lid. Shake well. Set to one side.

Salad

1 cup	sliced fresh mushrooms (or more)	250 mL
2 Tbsp.	drained pickled capers	30 mL
10 oz.-1 lb.	fresh spinach or romaine	400-500 g

Tear, wash and pat dry in towel any combination of spinach and romaine. Add mushrooms and capers. Cover and chill.

To Serve: Shake dressing. Toss into salad only enough dressing to coat greens. Taste and toss in more dressing if necessary. Serve immediately.

Best Spinach Or Romaine And Apple Salad

Serves 6

Tart with cheese, croutons and bacon. Make dressing early in day and chill. Prepare salad up to one hour before serving and chill.

Dressing

1/3 cup	safflower oil	*100 mL*
1/3 cup	cider vinegar	*100 mL*
3/4 tsp.	salt	*4 mL*
2 tsp.	sugar	*10 mL*
1 tsp.	Worcestershire sauce	*5 mL*
	1 large clove garlic - crushed	
1/3 cup	crumbled blue cheese	*100 mL*

Combine ingredients in jar with lid. Shake well. Chill.

Salad

	5 slices bacon	
1 cup	herbed croutons	*250 mL*
	1 red apple - diced with peel on	
	2 hard-boiled eggs - sliced	
1/4 cup	chopped green onion	*75 mL*
10 oz.-1 lb.	fresh spinach or romaine	*400-500 mL*

Fry bacon until crisp and then drain, crumble and chill. Chop apples into salad bowl, add eggs and onion, cover all with washed and dried spinach. Cover and chill.

To Serve: Shake dressing. Toss into salad. Toss in bacon. Sprinkle croutons over. Serve immediately.

A recipe I devised when we lived in Athens. I vividly remember those sweet Greek salads.

My Greek Salad

Serves 8 to 10 (halve recipe for 4 to 5)

For this salad I use Greek *'Kalamata* olive oil. It's aromatic, thick and, with the herbs, makes a dressing soft on your tongue. Concoct dressing early in day.

Dressing

1½ cups	olive oil (preferably Greek *'Kalamata* brand)	*375 mL*
1/2 cup	red wine vinegar with garlic	*125 mL*
2 tsp.	salt	*10 mL*
1/2 tsp.	pepper	*2 mL*
1 tsp.	dried leaf oregano	*5 mL*
1/2-1 tsp.	dried leaf basil	*2-5 mL*
	4 large cloves garlic - crush through garlic press into oil.	

Combine all ingredients in jar with lid. Chill to "marinate." Bring to room temperature to serve, and shake well."

Salad

	4 to 6 slices bacon - optional	
1/4-1/2 cup	Parmesan cheese (I use freshly grated cheese from my Greek deli	*75-125 mL*
1/2-1 lb.	any white cheese (e.g. feta, Lancashire, Gloucester, Cheshire) -cut into large chunks	*250-450 g*
1/2 lb.	fresh mushrooms - slice thick	*250 g*
	2 avocados - slice into thick chunks	

54

or

1 can drained sliced artichoke hearts

4 green onions - chop

lots fresh parsley - wash, dry, chop

14 oz.   1/2 to 1 can drained,   *398 mL*
      pitted halved black olives

or

Greek olives from your local
     delicatessen

2 to 3 medium tomatoes into eighths

or

10 to 12 cherry tomatoes halved

2 heads romaine

Fry bacon until crisp, drain, crumble and chill.   Grate Parmesan and reserve.   Cut all other ingredients into large salad bowl. Tear lettuce into bite-sized pieces, wash, dry and arrange in bowl. Chill.

Shake dressing well. Toss and pour just enough into salad to well-moisten the leaves, but not sog (watch this! Olive oil sneakily sops into your salad before you know it!) Toss in optional bacon. Toss in some Parmesan; use just enough to subtly flavor the salad, so taste while adding. Sprinkle rest over salad. Add tomatoes and serve.

Breads

I *refuse* to buy bread! With pride, I bake all our breadstuffs. This is a tradition of myself and many coast people. We value our self-reliant lifestyle.

However, I admit I'm biased against quick or synthetic foods. I take care to use wholesome wheat products in my breads. Similarly, friends and distant neighbors enjoy their baking, regarding it as a creative use of their time. Here, our health is vital. With no medical service nearby, we're responsible for sustaining ourselves. We have to be conscious of nutrition.

I like the soothing, physical rhythms of breadmaking. Pound, knead, fold. LIke the soft melody of a flute, baking calms me.

Although I prefer thick, dark breads, my curiosity and dislike of routine lead me constantly to pursue new varieties. By 10 a.m. when we breakfast, the lodge wafts wheat aromas over Lull Bay, I've got a couple of loaves cooling on the table; hungry people boat home. Ferociously, I prowl in my apron uniform, guarding my "creation" until everyone arrives. Homemade bread is an inlet breakfast ritual, to be savored without haste.

I prefer to prepare most of my breads and dishes ahead of mealtime - early in the day. Not for the sake of perfect controlled organization, but to slowly and completely savor the process involved. To all appearances, I seem to arrange a methodical routine of timed cookery stages:

6 a.m. Preparation of dinner salad.

7 a.m. Do dessert for dinner.

8-10 a.m. Breakfast cookery. Noon is main course preparation and by 1 or 2 p.m., bread or accompaniment dishes are under way. Much of this is, in fact, timed to coincide with our generator electricity.

Primarily, by preparing early, cooking becomes a musical dance - an orchestrated flowing activity at the center of which ... I'm tranquil. Creating without plan.

Finally, when my meal is done ahead, I have time to settle; balance my physical energy.

By mealtime, I'll be ready. Poised to culminate the dance without tension or haste.

Cinnamon Coffee Bread

Makes 2 "no-knead" loaves
Fluffy, sweet, crunchy with cornflakes. Best served warm at breakfast, brunch, or "tea-time." Prepare early in day up to 4 hours before serving, or make the night before and leave to rise in fridge overnight.

1 cup	warm water	250 mL
2 pkg. (2 Tbsp.)	*Fleischmann's* active dry yeast	30 mL
3 cups	all-purpose flour	750 mL
2½ tsp.	salt	12 mL
1/2 cup	sugar	125 mL
1/2 cup	soft shortening	125 mL
1 tsp.	vanilla	5 mL
	2 eggs	

In small bowl combine yeast and water. Let stand 10 minutes then stir to dissolve. Sift dry ingredients into large bowl, cut in shortening then beat in the yeast mixture, vanilla and eggs. Beat 2 minutes, medium speed. Scrape dough into center as you beat. Cover and let rise in warm place until bubbly and doubled (1 to 1½ hours).

Topping

1/2 cup	crushed cornflakes	125 mL
1 tsp.	cinnamon	5 mL
1/2 cup	sugar	125 mL
3 Tbsp.	melted margarine or butter	45 mL

While dough is rising, combine topping ingredients in small bowl and set aside.

Grease two 9''x 5''x 3'' loaf pans. Stir down bread dough and spread evenly in the pans. Divide cornflake topping evenly between pans. Spread to cover batter. Using fingers, press dents into dough, right to bottom of pans. Let rise until doubled (1 to 1½ hours, or overnight in fridge, covered). If risen in fridge, bring to room temperature next day (190° C.).
Bake 375° F., (190°C.) 20 or 30 minutes or until golden and feels 'done' when pressed. Cool in pans on rack 10 minutes. Then turn out on rack.

From Aunt Dot I learned all my basic values in cooking. She's simply my kind hearted, Baptist Auntie, known in her neighborhood for nourishing, tasty cooking. I suspect Aunt Dot equates her meals with love. Generously, she gives both. Aunt Dot's kitchen is a seasonal haven for us. During our hectic "Spring Buy" for the resort, we always stop at Aunt Dot's in Nanaimo for a family meal. This is one of the rare times I allow myself to gorge on food: Dot's sweet garden vegetables, buttery pies, and thick soups. And then, there's her ultimate of biscuits.

Aunt Dot's Crusty Cheese Biscuits

Makes 12 to 14

Very quick and easy, these biscuits make an excellent base for "Eggs Benedict" (See recipe p. 25)
Pre-heat oven to 425°F. (220°C)

2 cups	all-purpose flour (or half whole wheat flour)	500 mL
1½ tsp.	cream of tartar	7 mL
1 tsp.	baking soda	5 mL
1 tsp.	salt	5 mL
2 Tbsp.	brown sugar	30 mL
1/4 cup	soft margarine or butter (Dot uses butter)	75 mL
1 cup	old sharp cheddar cheese — coarsely grated	250 mL
3/4-1 cup	milk	200-250 mL

Sift dry ingredients into large bowl. Knead in margarine until coarsely crumbled. Stir in cheese and slowly add just enough milk to make a batter thin enough to drop from a spoon (i.e., of "muffin dough" consistency). Stir just enough to mix. Cover large cookie sheet with foil and grease it. Drop 12 to 14 huge spoonfuls batter on cookie sheet. Bake 12 to 15 minutes. Serve hot. Delicious with butter, jam (I slather on Aunt Dot's crabapple), or honey.

Aunt Dot's Bran Muffins

Makes 12 huge!

I love these filling, wholesome muffins for breakfast. I heat them up, put out lots of butter, honey, and Aunt Dot's homemade crabapple or blackberry jam, and watch guests make a meal out of them. Any that are left, freeze, to be re-heated for unexpected snacks. See Dot's jam recipes at end of "Breads" section. Make up to one hour before serving.
Preheat oven to 400°F. (200°C)

2½ cups	flour (part whole wheat and part all-purpose)	625 mL
1½ tsp.	cream of tartar	7 mL
1 tsp.	baking soda	5 mL
1 tsp.	cinnamon	5 mL
1 tsp.	salt	5 mL
1 cup	whole natural bran	250 mL
1 cup	chopped dates	250 mL
1/2 cup	raisins	125 mL
1 cup	boiling water	250 mL
1/2 cup	brown sugar	125 mL
	or	
1/3 cup	honey	100 mL
1/2 tsp.	baking soda	2 mL
1 cup	buttermilk — (or 7/8 cup (225 mL) milk plus 2 Tbsp. (30 mL) lemon juice or vinegar)	250 mL
1 tsp.	vanilla	5 mL
	2 eggs	
3/4 cup	oil (Aunt Dot uses melted whipped butter)	200 mL

Sift first five ingredients into large bowl. Add bran. Set aside. In small bowl, combine dates, raisins, boiling water, sugar, and baking soda. Let sit 5-10 minutes. Meanwhile, in medium bowl combine buttermilk, vanilla, eggs, oil. Beat well. To sifted ingredients in large bowl, stir in the sugar and date mixture and the buttermilk mixture. Grease 12 large muffin cups. Pour in batter right to tops, mounding high. Don't worry if it overflows onto pan. Bake 20 minutes. Let cool in pan 10 minutes, then remove muffins to racks to cool.

Carrot-Pineapple Muffins

Makes 11 to 12

Huge, hearty. Excellent for brunch.

Muffins freeze well. Make up to 45 minutes before serving.
Pre-heat oven to 350ºF. (180ºC.).

2 cups	coarsely grated carrots	500 mL
1 cup	crushed pineapple with juice	250 mL
3 cups	flour — half white, half whole wheat	750 mL
1 cup	sugar	250 mL
2 tsp.	baking powder	10 mL
1½ tsp.	salt	7 mL
2 tsp.	baking soda	10 mL
2 tsp.	cinnamon	10 mL
	4 eggs	
2 tsp.	pure vanilla extract	10 mL
1 cup	vegetable oil (I use safflower)	250 mL

Sift dry ingredients together. Beat together oil, eggs and vanilla and stir into flour mixture. Add carrots and pineapple. Stir just until all blended.

Pour into greased muffin pan, mounding *above* the tops.
Bake 25 minutes.
Cool in pan 10 minutes, then turn out onto rack.

Quick Irish Soda Bread

Makes two round loaves

Quite heavy and crunchy. Delicious with honey or jam, or as an accompaniment to any of the soups. Make up to one hour before serving.
Preheat oven to 350°F (180°C.)

4 cups	whole wheat flour	1 L
2 tsp.	baking soda	10 mL
2 tsp.	salt	10 mL
1/4 cup	cracked wheat	75 mL
1/2 cup	wheat germ	125 mL
1/2 lb.	margarine	250 g
	2 eggs	

| 1/2 cup | water | 125 mL |
| 2 cups | buttermilk (or 1-¾ cup (450 mL) milk plus ¼ cup (50 mL) lemon juice or vinegar) | 500 mL |

Sift flour, soda and salt into large bowl and stir in cracked wheat and wheat germ. Cut in margarine. In a small bowl, beat eggs and water; add buttermilk. Stir liquids into flour mixture. Stir dough until everything is well blended.

Spread foil-wrap over long cookie sheet and grease foil. Spoon dough into two high mounds. Leave lots of space around each on foil. Sprinkle lots of flour over dough. Cut an 'X' into top of each. Bake 40 to 45 minutes. Remove from foil and cool on rack.

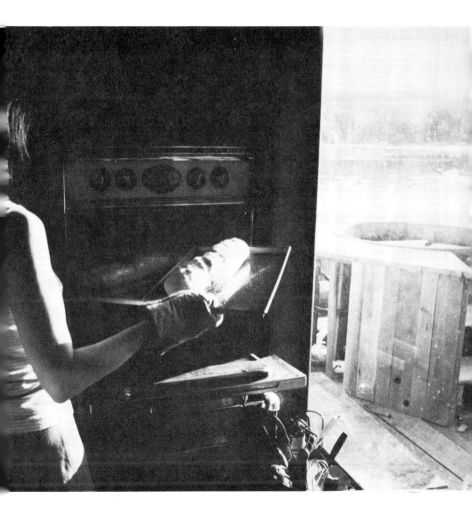

Symbolically, Klinaklini River is the graveyard of Knight Inlet; birthplace of the coast mountains. Here, the inlet dwindles its power into the river. The river winds its life through the mountains to disappear in dry flatlands — B.C.'s Cariboo.

In small ways, I defy and humanize this natural immensity. Narrowing the scope, I define my space here with a lodge, boats, people, friendships, a kitchen, even these cinnamon buns.

Thick with raisins and rum glaze, these buns keep people full during our rare "all-day" trips down the inlet. Klinaklini River is too far for guests to explore so they stop off at glaciers part way. Out come the leftover buns, chunks of smoked salmon, fresh crab. My daily "snack bag" for the men.

Klinaklini Cinnamon Buns

Makes 20 huge!

Make the night before. Leave to rise in fridge or make at least 3 hours before serving.

In small bowl combine:

1 cup	warm water	250 mL
2 Tbsp.	yeast	30 mL
1 tsp.	sugar	5 mL
1 cup	milk	250 mL
1/2 cup	sugar	125 mL
1 Tbsp.	salt	15 mL
	2 eggs	
5-7 cups	sifted all-purpose flour	1¼-1½ L
1/4 cup	melted margarine	75 mL

In a small bowl, combine water, yeast and 1 tsp.(5 mL) sugar. Stir, let stand 10 minutes to dissolve. Meanwhile, in small saucepan, combine milk, remaining sugar and salt. Heat to lukewarm. Remove from heat. In large bowl beat eggs and dissolved yeast. Stir in warm milk. Stir in 2 cups (500 mL) flour and beat well with electric mixer. Beat in one more cup (250 mL) white flour, then gradually stir in two more cups (500 mL) flour and margarine. Knead 5 to 8 minutes, adding up to 2 more cups flour until dough is firm but still slightly sticky. Place in greased bowl. Grease top. Cover. Let rise 1 hour until doubled.

Filling

3/4 cup	brown sugar	200 mL
1½ tsp.	cinnamon	7 mL
1-2 cups	(lots) - dark raisins	250-500 mL

Stir together in one bowl. Set to one side.

Melt and set to one side:

1/3 cup	margarine	100 mL

When dough is doubled, punch down, turn out on floured surface; knead a few times. Roll out into two 12"x 9" rectangles. Brush each rectangle with half the melted margarine. Sprinkle each rectangle with half the cinnamon, sugar, raisin mixture.

Roll up from the short (9") end. Pinch edges to seal. Cut each roll into 10 even slices. Arrange slices in two well-buttered 13"x 9"x 2" baking pans (10 slices or buns per pan). Slices should resemble large flat spirals. Try to leave some space around each bun. Cover.

Let rise overnight in fridge or rise in warm place one hour until doubled.

The next morning bring buns to room temperature one hour before baking.

Glaze

3 Tbsp.	margarine	45 mL
2 cups	sifted icing sugar	500 mL
2 Tbsp.	hot, strong coffee	30 mL
1/4 tsp.	maple extract	1 mL
1/4 tsp.	rum extract	1 mL

Melt margarine in medium saucepan and stir in the dry ingredients. Set aside.

Thirty minutes before serving, pre-heat oven to 400° F. (200° C.) Bake buns 20 minutes until golden. Meanwhile, arrange two long cookie sheets on counter. When buns are baked, immediately invert onto cookie sheets. Quickly, evenly, spread glaze over hot buns. It'll soak in. Best served warm, but are good re-heated in foil. (Glaze will run, though!)

Beth and Will live at Freshwater Bay on Swanson Island, near the mouth of Knight Inlet. A radiant, blond viking of a woman is Beth. Whether chopping wood, cod-jigging, clearing their land, chasing Will's Bavarian boars from the garden, photographing the land's beauty, playing her mandolin, or writing articles for city magazines, Beth's warm vitality embraces life.

Beth got this bread recipe from her Swedish grandmother who used to bake each bun in tiny, loaf-shaped molds.

Beth's Bran Rolls

Makes 16.

Huge, yeasty rolls. Make the night before and leave in fridge to rise.

2 Tbsp.	yeast	30 mL
1 cup	lukewarm water	250 mL
1/2 cup	margarine	125 mL
1/2 cup	sugar	125 mL
1 cup	whole natural bran	250 mL
1 Tbsp.	salt	15 mL
1 cup	boiling water	250 mL
	2 eggs	
1 cup	whole wheat flour	250 mL
1/4 cup	wheat germ	75 mL
5¼ cups	all-purpose flour (or more)	I L plus 325 mL

In small bowl, combine yeast and warm water. In large bowl, combine margarine, sugar, bran and salt. Add boiling water and let cool until warm. Beat eggs and add to bran mixture. Add yeast mixture. Stir in 1 cup (250 mL) each of whole wheat and all-purpose flours, add wheat germ. Beat 2 minutes with electric mixer. Stir in remaining flour until easy to knead. Turn out on board. Knead 10 minutes. Place in greased bowl; grease top of dough. Cover and chill in fridge overnight, or at least 4 hours.

Two hours before serving time, remove dough from fridge. Punch down. Roll out into two rectangles. Roll up into two thick strands. Cut into sixteen equal portions. Shape into rolls.

Place in two greased 9"x 9" pans. Let rise 1-1½ hours in warm place. Bake 425° F. (220 ° C.) 20 minutes. Turn out on wire racks. Best served warm, or re-heated in foil, later. Keep well-wrapped: these buns get tough and dry quickly.

Bones Bay: A huge deserted mausoleum of a cannery on the coast. The cannery itself consists of echoing, windowless buildings and empty, cramped hutches which once house the Chinese laborers. Behind lies the old, Indian graveyard where nearby tribes left their smallpox-sick to die. In the '40s, Bones Bay was a fishing city of activity. Local seiners and trollers stored nets and gear in the cannery loft. Chinese, Finnish and Indian laborers gutted and packed the fleet's catch. People working together, fishing together, clearing the land for gardens, drinking and socializing together in their boats: bound by a common industry. Today Bones Bay is a silent ghost town, cared for by a local hand-logging family. Yet an aura of past energy still hovers over those brooding pilings.

I got this excellent bun recipe from Marilyn Berry. Marilyn caretakes Bones Bay and turns out tasty home-cooking for whoever boats up to her wharf. She and Bill, her husband, still grow raspberries and vegetables in the old cannery gardens and raise their own chickens. These products, plus local seafoods, tide them over between monthly boat trips to the supermarket in Alert Bay, (our closest fishing town).

All Marilyn's breads are homemade, chewy, grainy. They rise slowly over her cannery oil stove. Often, I'm there for the baking -just sitting in Marilyn's kitchen at Bill's hand-finished fir table.

A glass of Bill's blackberry wine, a cup of Marilyn's dried-mint tea, some Bones Bay buns or sourdough, and good conversation.....

Bones Bay Buns

Makes 16

Try to make the dough the night before or at *least* six hours before serving.

2 Tbsp.	yeast	30 mL
1 tsp.	sugar	5 mL
1/4 cup	lukewarm water	75 mL
2 cups	milk	500 mL
3 Tbsp.	shortening or margarine	45 mL
	2 beaten eggs	
1/2 cup	sugar	125 mL
1½ Tbsp.	salt	20 mL
4-6 cups	all-purpose flour	1 L plus
		250- 500 mL
1 cup	whole wheat flour	250 mL
1/4 cup	wheat germ	75 mL

Combine yeast, sugar and water. Let stand in warm place 10-15 minutes. Stir once to dissolve. Warm milk and margarine in saucepan, add eggs, sugar and salt. Sift 2 cups (500 mL) all-purpose flour into large bowl and add yeast and milk mixtures. Beat with electric mixer 1 minute. Add whole wheat flour and wheat germ, beat 1-2 minutes. Stir in 3-4 more cups flour, or enough for soft dough. Reserve some of last cup to knead in. Knead 10 minutes in large bowl. Grease top of dough. Cover and place in fridge overnight, or let rise in fridge *at least* 4 hours.

Two hours before serving, punch dough down. Form into ball, cut in half, and roll each half into two long rectangles. Roll each rectangle up into two thick strands, tucking seams under. Cut each strand into 8 equal portions. Foil-line and grease two 8"x 8" cake pans. Shape dough portions into rough, lumpy balls. Place 8 in each pan, leaving space between balls. Cover. Let rise 1-1½ hours, or until doubled.

Bake 375° F. (190° C.) 20 minutes. Turn out onto cake racks. Serve hot, buttered, or cool and re-warm in foil.

Ed was our very first fishing guide. Through the struggling years of the resort's growth, we could always count on our friend Ed to fly out to the coast from Toronto for each summer season.

When we started the business, Ed was so scared of bungling his "guide" role, he took notes. He wrote out all the lures and when to use them. He painstakingly studied books on knots. Then he graduated to practicing boat-landings against the wharf, and memorizing demonstrations on "how to gut" fish. I often think of Ed when I see herons. In fact, my pal, "Cristopher Crane" particularly resembles Ed. Patiently Cristopher stands, poised on one long, boney leg, watching the bay. His body reflects the graceful length and calm reserve of Ed.

Today, many guests still ask after Ed. His shy kindness and quiet love of the land endeared him to people. This recipe was his masterpiece, a bread he baked often here in the inlet and home in Toronto.

Ed's Bread

Makes two huge, wheat loaves

Make at least four and a half hours before serving.

1 Tbsp.	yeast	15 mL
2 tsp.	sugar	10 mL
1/2 cup	lukewarm water	125 mL
1 Tbsp.	toasted sesame or poppy seeds	15 mL
3 Tbsp.	brown sugar	45 mL
1/4 cup	molasses	75 mL
2 Tbsp.	vegetable oil	30 mL
3 cups	lukewarm water	750 mL
4 cups	sifted all-purpose flour	1 L
5 tsp.	salt	25 mL
5-6 cups	whole wheat flour, or more	1 L plus 250-500 mL

including

1/4 cup	wheat germ as part of the 5 cups flour	75 mL

Dissolve yeast and 2 tsp. (10 mL) sugar in 1/2 cup (125 mL) water, let stand 10 minutes. Stir once. In large bowl, mix seeds, brown sugar, molasses, oil, all-purpose flour, salt and water. Add yeast mixture and beat 2-3 minutes with electric mixer. Stir in whole wheat flour and wheat germ.

Knead 10 minutes, keading in the sixth cup (final 250 mL) of flour. Place dough in greased bowl, turn to grease top, cover, let rise 1½ hours or until doubled. Then punch down, divide dough in half, shape into 2 loaves, and place in two greased 9"x5"x3" loaf pans. Grease tops, sprinkle sesame or poppy seeds over, cover, let rise 1½ hours or until doubled. Bake 350° F. (180° C.), 1 hour, turn out on racks to cool. Delicious warm

Cornmeal And Molasses Bread
Makes two thick, filling loaves

This, plus Janet's "Sennebec Hill" bread, are favorite loaves. People, especially Canadians, often request these breads, perhaps because we're less familiar with cornmeal baking up here. Good with any of the soups or with honey or jam for breakfast, or to complement seafood dinners. Make early in day or up to 4½ hours before serving. Can make dough the night before and leave to rise in fridge overnight.

1/2 cup	cornmeal	125 mL
2 cups	boiling water	500 mL
1/2 cup	warm water	125 mL
2 pkg. (2 Tbsp.)	Fleischmann's active dry yeast	30 mL
1/3 cup	softened margarine	125 mL
1/2 cup	molasses	125 mL
2½ cups	whole wheat flour	625 mL
1 Tbsp.	salt	15 mL
2 cups	all-purpose flour	500 mL

Stir cornmeal into boiling water and let stand until cool (30 minutes or so). Stir occasionally - it'll be thick. Meanwhile in a small bowl combine yeast and warm water, let stand 10 minutes, then stir to dissolve. Add margarine and molasses.

In a large bowl combine whole wheat flour and salt and beat in yeast and cornmeal mixtures for 2 minutes at medium speed. Add 1/2 cup (125 mL) all-purpose flour and beat 1-2 minutes more. Stir in rest of flour to make softish dough.

Knead 10 minutes (may have to knead in 1/2 cup (125 mL) more flour to prevent sticking). Place in greased bowl, grease top of dough. Cover. Rise in warm place until doubled (1½ hours). Then punch down. Divide and shape into two loaves. Place in two greased 9"x 5"x 3" loaf pans. Cover. Let rise in warm place until doubled (1½ hours) or rise in the fridge overnight and then bring to room temperature the next day.

Bake 375° F. (190° C.), 45 minutes. Turn out onto rack and cool. Best served warm. After first day, reheat slices in foil.

In "The Black Hole" lurk "Einstein" and "Schweitzer"! "The black hole" - euphemish for our young guides' unique room. Cramped with sleeping bags; crowded with fish gear, lures, flashers, hootchies, downriggers and unrecognizable inventions; reeking of stale beer, stale socks, fumes from the generator; adorned with gracefully dangling underwear, the "black hole" somehow survives. Perhaps due to psychology books dumped alongside Playboy magazines, perhaps due to sheer trust in chaos....

There, Einstein and Schweitzer retire. Tim - our Einstein - the intellectual; Martin - our Schweitzer - the humanist. Together a powerful team.

There's conflict. Tim's intrigued with information. Problems and solutions challenge him: "Twenty ways to fix the downriggers; ten approaches to re-organizing resort schedules." Martin prefers to joke with the guests and discuss their lives. Schweitzer and Einstein examine each other's viewpoints, argue, learn from each other. They're good friends.

Both guides are indispensable to the resort. Responsible, conscientious, they subsist on four to five hours of sleep a night, drag themselves out fishing for 3:30 a.m. "dawn patrols," summon enough energy to clean fish at midnight after evening fishing, and still take time to relax with guests in the hot tub. On "changeover days," they good-naturedly help me out: vacuuming guests' rooms, unloading my groceries, washing down the lodge windows in between cleaning their gory boats; raiding the crab traps for me.

Comic company, this duo. One night, Einstein and Schweitzer sacrificed two hours of sleep to steal John's "magic box." A ransom note was devised. In return for John's depth-sounder cum fish-detector, both guides wanted music in the lodge. No music - no "magic box." Martin and Tim, ingenious thieves, won.

In many ways, they sustain our lodge. I love them. Schweitzer and Einstein are youth and joy in Lull Bay.

This is their favorite bread.

Rye Beer Bread

Makes two long French loaves.

Delicious with smoked salmon pate (see recipe p 85), hot, thick soups (Will's Borscht, p. 34) or as a snack along with ceviche (p. 93) or cheeses.

Make early in day - up to four hours before serving. Or make night before and leave dough to rise in fridge overnight.

2 pkg. (2 Tbsp.)	Fleischmann's active dry yeast	30 mL
1/2 cup	lukewarm water	125 mL
2½ cups	beer	625 mL
1/3 cup	margarine or shortening	100 mL
1/2 cup	dark molasses	125 mL
1 Tbsp.	salt	15 mL
1 tsp.	caraway seed	5 mL
5 cups	rye flour	1 L plus 250 mL
3 cups	all-purpose flour	750 mL

Dissolve yeast in water. Let stand 10 minutes then stir to dissolve.

Heat beer in saucepan until bubbly. Remove from heat and stir in margarine until melted. Add molasses, salt and caraway seed, and cool to lukewarm.

In large bowl, combine yeast and beer mixtures. Add 2 cups (500 mL) rye flour and beat 2 minutes at medium speed. Add 1 more cup (250 mL) rye flour, beat 2 minutes, then stir in last 2 cups (500 mL) rye flour. Finally stir in all-purpose flour.

Stir into ball of firmish dough. Knead 10 minutes (adding 1 cup more all-purpose flour if necessary). Place in greased bowl, butter top of dough. Cover, let rise in warm place until doubled (1½ hours) or let rise in fridge overnight. Then bring to room temperature next day.

When doubled, punch dough down. Cut in half. Shape each half into long French loaf. Place each loaf on greased cookie sheet. Slash tops to 1/4" (1 cm.) depth. Brush tops with mixture of 1 egg beaten with 1 Tbsp. (15 mL) water. Reserve some of the egg mix for later. Let stand in warm place until doubled (1½ hours). Brush lightly with rest of egg. Sprinkle poppy seeds over.

Bake 350° F. (180° C), 40 to 45 minutes, until deep brown and sounds hollow when tapped. Cool on racks.

Older people have a valued place in coast communities. They're respected and referred to for their knowledge; they often work, despite age, at jobs or crafts that involve a lifetime of developed skill. They're a colorful addition to community gatherings with their mature perspective of coast history and their interesting stories.

My 70 year old friend, Janet, is one such. Janet's a philosopher in disguise. But you have to sneak up on the quality. Behind her humorous homilies, twinkling green eyes, and snappy, succinct wit lies a wise, compassionate perception of people.

Energizing company and imaginative cook, Janet's usually got at least two projects or businesses "bubbling" in Vancouver. She loves a challenge: even substituted for me on "days off" one summer. That took sixteen hours a day of physical work, but Janet breezed through it (sometimes I merely surive it!).

Here's what Janet describes as "a standard New England bread," which means it's got a delicious, wheat-sweet taste, and it's one of my favorites. "Sennebec Hill" refers, I think, to the coastal Virginia are where Janet "discovered" this recipe.

Janet's "Sennebec Hill" Bread

Makes two 9"x 5"x 3" loaves

Prepare four hours before serving, or can make dough night before and leave to rise in fridge.

2 Tbsp.	yeast (I use *Fleischmann's* active dry)	30 mL
2 cups	very warm water	500 mL
1/2 cup	molasses (light)	125 mL
	2 eggs	
1 Tbsp.	salt	15 mL
1/3 cup	oil (safflower is best)	100 mL
1 cup	dry skim milk powder	250 mL
1/2 cup	long-cooking rolled oats	125 mL
1/2 cup	yellow cornmeal	125 mL
1/2 cup	wheat germ	125 mL
1 cup	rye flour	250 mL
2 cups	whole wheat flour	500 mL
2-3 cups	all-purpose flour	500-700 mL

Dissolve yeast in water, then add all ingredients except flours and beat well at low speed with electric mixer. Gradually add rye flour and whole wheat flour and continue beating 2 minutes. Stir in all-purpose flour, enough to form soft but kneadable dough. May knead in up to 1 more cup (250 mL). Knead dough 8 to 10 minutes. Place in large greased bowl. Grease top. Cover. Let rise 1½ hours or until doubled. Then punch down, shape into two loaves, place in two greased 9"x 5"x 3" loaf pans. Butter tops and sprinkle sesame seeds or poppy seeds over. Cover. Let rise in fridge overnight, or 1½ hours in warm place until doubled.

Final Preparation: If risen in fridge, bring loaves to room temperature for 1 hour before baking. Preheat oven to 375° F. (190° C.), and bake 40 minutes. Turn out on rack. Very tender bread with lots of texture and "chew."

Quick Corn Loaf

Makes one large loaf

Take 10 minutes to prepare. Delicious with bean dishes, fish or meat dinners and stews. Prepare 80 to 90 minutes before serving. Preheat oven to 425° F. (220° C.).

1 2/3 cups	all-purpose flour	425 mL
2/3 cup	white sugar	175 mL
1 Tbsp. plus		
2 tsp.	baking powder	20 mL—25 mL
1½ tsp.	salt	7 mL
1 2/3 cups	regular fine yellow cornmeal	425 mL
1/3 cup	melted butter or margarine	100 mL
	2 large eggs	
1 2/3 cups	milk	425 mL

Sift dry ingredients and cornmeal into large bowl. Beat eggs with milk. Add with melted butter to flour mixture. Stir just until all blended. Pour batter into well-greased 9½"x 5½"x 3½" loaf pan.

Bake 425° F. (220° C.) - 50-60 minutes, covering with foil halfway through baking time. When tests done in middle, cool in pan on rack - 10 minutes. Turn out and slice.

Jams & Jellies

For the past two years, John Dolmedge's tug *Service-Nine* has towed *Sailcone* up Knight Inlet to Lull Bay. This year, we pulled out at 3 a.m. after anxiously "waiting out" a southeast gale and numerous weather reports. My pal - photographer Beth (see "Beth's Bran Buns" in Breads section) and I sipped strong Espresso at the dining table as gray mountains glided past the windows. At dawn, Will (of "Will's Roosian Borsch" pg. 34) boated Beth out to photograph *Service-Nine* pulling the whole resort... into a silver sunrise.

By 10 a.m., a warm day, we floated quietly in Lull Bay. Our

"tuggers" seeped their fatigue into the wharfside hot tub. For breakfast, I served everyone a quiche, Janet's "Sennebec Hill" bread (see Breads section), and this salal jelly. The recipe has been passed down through the Dolmedge family to John, at his Bones Bay home.

Service-Nine Salal Berry Jelly

A strong, delicious grape-like jam or jelly. Serve with hot breads, or as a relish with chicken or pork.

Salal berries grow wild and blue on the coast. You need to pick a lot to make this jelly. Sometimes they can be very bitter.

Very simple!

- *Cover* the amount of berries you've picked (hopefully a *lot*) with water. *Cook* 10 minutes, and crush or mash berries while they cook.

- *Add* chopped vegetable marrow if they seem too concentrated or bitter-tasting.

- Strain berries through jelly bag and reserve juice.

- To each cup of juice, *add* 1 cup (250 mL) sugar. Add lemon juice to taste.

- Boil the juice - sugar mixture until it jells (forms separate drops on spoon).

- Seal in jars.

Aunt Dot's Crabapple - Honey Jelly

Aunt Dot makes this red jelly for the resort. The crabapples flourish in her Nanaimo back yard.

Jelly is tart, red, rich with honey taste. Ordinary crabapples may be used with great success. It's best to use a juicer with this recipe, though you can do without. You can also use sugar instead of honey.

- *Wash* unpeeled fruit (any amount). *Remove* stems and flower ends and cut apples in half. Put two-thirds of the apples through a juicer to extract the juice, *or* add water to just cover the apples; boil and then sieve out the juice. Pour juice into deep, heavy pot (*not* aluminum). Add remaining one-third apples to juice.

-*Boil* till apples tender enough to mash, then continue boiling 5 to 10 minutes.

- *Pour* into jelly bag or several thicknesses cheesecloth which have been wrung out in hot water. Allow juice to run through into a container.

- For each cup (250 mL) of juice, *add* 2/3 cup (175 mL) liquid honey *or* 3/4 cup (200 mL) sugar.

- *Boil* until syrup reaches "jellying stage" (Aunt Dot tests this by waiting till syrup forms separate drops which don't run together on spoon).

- *Pour* into glasses; allow to cool and set. Seal with wax.

Honey Blackberry or Crabapple Jam

Make this jam with sugar or honey.

The Blackberry Jam

-*Wash* berries (any amount you have); place in deep, heavy pot.

- *Mash* berries just enough to cook in their own juice.

-*Cook* until berries tender enough to be put through sieve. Reserve the pulp.

The Apple Jam

Make as above by washing and de-stemming apples. Place in pot, add water to just cover, boil until tender enough to put through sieve. Reserve the pulp.

To continue both Blackberry and Apple Jams:

Measure out a mixture of combined juice and some pulp, adding 2/3 cup (175 mL) liquid honey or 3/4 to 1 cup (200 - 250 mL) sugar to each 1 cup (250 mL) of fruit or berry mixture.

Bring to rolling boil until it "sets" on spoon (approx. 30 - 40 minutes). Stir while bringing to boil (prevents burning), but don't continue to stir while jam boils.

Pour into jars and seal.

Seafood

Since the resort lives fishing, I've concentrated on developing seafood recipes. Originally, I noticed that guests were interested in *all* aspects of resort life: they asked me to devise recipes with them for their fresh catch. They leaped to help our guides lift the crab pots. Intrigued, they watched me skin octopus.

They'd even research our maps! As seriously as they'd peruse a contract, guests studied local landmarks and areas to fish. Even now, aggressive businessmen still line up on the wharf to cast for bullheads. Sometimes it becomes a derby, with administrators and professionals competing to hook the most sablefish.

In honor of such dedication, I've titled some of the seafood recipes after the inlet's best "fishing holes."

Minstrel Island lies fifteen miles west of us, a turbulent, thirty-five minute boat trip down Knight Inlet. There reside the bulk of this area's populace: three families, a scruffy horse named "Bridey," two mongrels, a flock of sterile chickens, the community hall, the old Swallow Inn, and the woody general store.

Minstrel is, and was, the hub of local fishing. Here, all the seiners traditionally congregate at the government wharf during herring season. Here, local families boat in for dances and communal dinners. In the '20s, a band of wandering minstrels did, in fact, serenade loggers at the then "booming" island town.

We built our new lodge at Minstrel, so I got to know its green, woodland trails and local cod-jigging holes. Uppermost in my memory of Minstrel, though, is the smell: dank mud, seaweed odors of the tide flats (great clamming!), the sharp, rich scents of pine forest and alder groves. I relished every chance, there, to simply walk and savor. Since we lived at the wharf, any movement on land seemed a luxury. Usually I'd stroll to my favorite view: high on the cliffs, looking out over "The Blowhole" and Cutter Cove, past Knight Inlet, to one distant, blue mountain.

Minstrel Seafood Crepes

Serves 8 to 10

Chicken and Shrimp crepes *or* Crab and Shrimp crepes: invented during a winter sojourn at the Minstrel Island wharf.

Crepes excellent with minted peas, or veggie crudites and a dip, or with light spinach or broccoli or lettuce soup and French bread. Also delicious with spinach-stuffed tomatoes (see my Vegetables section). Early in day, make the crepes and filling.

Crepes *(Makes 20-30 crepes - 2 or 3 per person).*

1½ cups	sifted all-purpose flour	375 mL
	2 eggs	
1/4 tsp.	salt	1 mL
2½ cups	milk	625 mL
1 Tbsp.	chopped fresh parsley	15 mL
1 Tbsp.	chopped fresh chives	15 mL
1/2 tsp.	dried leaf tarragon	2 mL
3 Tbsp.	melted butter	45 mL

Combine flour, eggs and salt in medium bowl. Gradually whisk in milk. Strain. Add remaining ingredients. Heat a 6" to 7" heavy iron skillet. Keep lightly brushed with butter before cooking each crepe. Pour in *scant* 1/4 cup (75 mL) measure of batter. Quickly swirl to cover bottom of skillet. Cook until lightly browned. Then drop crepe, cooked side up, onto plate. Quickly drop back, uncooked side down, into hot skillet. Cook until lightly browned.

Turn out onto platter. Place small piece wax paper over. Repeat process with remaining crepes, keeping each separate with wax paper as you stack them.

Filling

3 Tbsp.	butter	45 mL
2 Tbsp.	fine-chopped scallions (green onions)	30 mL
1/3 cup	dry white wine	100 mL
1 Tbsp.	fine-chopped chives	15 mL
1 Tbsp.	fine-chopped parsley	15 mL
1/2 tsp.	dried leaf tarragon	2 mL
2 cups	flaked crabmeat (drained) *or* cooked pieces of chicken	500 mL
1 cup	chopped cooked shrimp (drained) salt and pepper to taste	250 mL

Melt butter, add scallions and saute 1 minute. Add wine. Reduce, (boil), all over high heat until only half the liquid remains. Add remaining ingredients, stir, heat briefly, then set aside.

Mornay Sauce *(Makes 3 cups or 750 mL)*

2 Tbsp.	butter	30 mL
3 Tbsp.	flour	45 mL
1-3/4 cup	milk	425 mL
1/3 cup	cream (or evaporated milk)	75 mL
1 cup	grated Swiss cheese	250 mL
	1 egg yolk	
1/8 tsp.	nutmeg	1 mL
	salt and pepper to taste	

Melt butter, stir in flour, add milk and cream. Heat to thicken, stirring constantly. Add cheese and stir until it melts. Bring mixture to boil. Stir in egg yolk, remove from heat and add seasonings. Set aside.

Stir half the Mornay Sauce into crab or chicken filling. Reserve half the sauce to spread over crepes. Divide crab or chicken filling into 16-20 equal portions, (one per crepe). Mound each portion evenly along bottom third of each crepe (do one at a time).

Roll up each crepe, placing in buttered 13"x 9"x 2" baking pan, or two 8"x 8"x 2" pans. Spread remaining sauce over rolled crepes.

Bake, uncovered, 425° F. (220° C.) 20 minutes or until hot through. Broil at last minute to brown tops (watch not to burn!). Serve.

Although J-C. cooks for a neighboring camp, he's also a pal. John's the friendly voice on our C-B, the closest neighbor to share jokes, exchange information, trade foods and recipes, and, occasionally, get together with over a meal. "Glendale calling Lull Bay," squawks the C-B, and I know John's "on."

When I think of John, I also picture Nicholas - his camp mutt: black, huge, cowardly and a mooch. Often, John boats over with Nick. While John and I sip tea, Nick suspiciously patrols the wharf, drools over the gut-bucket, and barks ferociously at Spencer the crow.

John typifies the kind of physical young men that love and survive this country. Enterprising, independent, respectful and careful of the land's resources, John makes his living here by hand-logging and alternately cooking and co-managing his resort. He works hard and does well.

For me, John's a reassuring presence in the inlet. When I almost severed my fingers, I could luckily boat over to "Dr." John for a patch job. When John's generator broke down, we offered our auxiliary replacement. In many small ways, we help each other out. We're each other's protection in the wilderness.

"John the Cook's"
Smoked Salmon

John's "old reliable" method.

These smoked fillets freeze well and can last you over a year. Have lots of fresh salmon - 10-60 lbs. (5-30 kg), depending on the size of your smoker. We use an old shed and hot plate with alder chips. John uses gutted fridges with slow-burning alder cut by his guides.

Fillet salmon in long, thin slabs with skin on. Marinate, covered, 12 hours or overnight, in:

Ratio of 1 cup (250 mL) brown sugar to 1/2 cup (125 mL) coarse salt. Double, quadruple, etc., amount of this recipe to cover approximately, all sides of the amount of salmon you have (for example, 5 lb. (2.5 kg) of brown sugar will usually do for 40 lb. (20 kg) of salmon).

Mix sugar and salt well in large bowl, according to the ration given above.

Arrange some of the fillets, skin down, to cover bottom of long, deep pan or water-proof box (we use styrofoam fish-cooling boxes for this). Spread marinade thickly over this bottom layer, arrange more fillets, skin down, on top, spread marinade over. Repeat this process until all fillets are stacked up and completely coated with marinade.

Cover and let stand 12 hours. Much liquid will accumulate. At end of 12 hours, pour this off. Smoke fish until well-flavored (1-3 days). You may have to bake fillets in oven to finish off the cooking process.

Silence shrouds Lull Bay.

It whispers and wraiths around valley mountains, it recedes into winding mysteries of coast inlets, it hulks and looms in our hills. Silence thickens and deepens with greendeep waves of ocean - forest.

In the lodge, we float to the pulse of ocean silence. Human murmurings, eagle shrieks, pumpings of marine toilet, whistling 5 a.m. kettle, squeaking baby swallows in the eaves: surface echoings to a silent harmony. Myriad noises rise and subside. Schlurfing waves, buzzing of plastic lettuce-dryer: snortings of mink and "Ollie the Otter," and seals. Ice clinks at the bar; birdsong quivers above shore. Poised; crystal sounds amidst stillness.

Silence in this country is alive! Soul music to me.

Smoked Salmon Pate

Makes 1½ cups. Recipe can be halved.

6 oz.		
(1¼ cup)	smoked salmon	250 g
2 Tbsp.	fresh lemon juice	30 mL
1/2 cup	melted butter	125 mL
1/2 cup	dairy sour cream	125 mL
1 Tbsp.	fresh dillweed OR	15 mL
1/2 tsp.	dried dillweed	3 mL dried
	pepper to taste	

In blender, blend salmon and lemon juice, add butter in a stream, then other ingredients. Refrigerate, covered, up to one week. Bring to room temperature 60 minutes before serving.

Delicious with crackers, biscuits, or "rye-beer bread". (recipe p.72).

85

Smoked Salmon Quiche

Makes one 10" pie - serves 4 to 8

For big groups, double recipes of seafood quiches and save a lot of time. Serve for brunch, lunch or dinner. Good with a green salad and French or corn bread.

	6 slices bacon	
4 oz.	can *Ortega* mild green chilis	*100 g*
1/4 cup	smoked salmon, (more for stronger smoked taste)	*75 mL*
1/4 lb.		
(1 cup)	Monterey Jack cheese	*250 mL*
1/4 lb.		
(1 cup)	mild cheddar cheese	*250 mL*
	4 eggs	
1½ cups	light cream or evaporated milk	*375 mL*
1 tsp.	salt	*5 mL*
	1 small onion - quartered	
1/2 tsp.	'fines herbes' or dried leaf marjoram	*2 mL*

Prepare pastry *(Aunt Dot's Butter Pastry - see recipe p. 132)*, pie plate and partially bake (10 minutes at 425° F. 220° C.). Cool.

Fry bacon until crisp, drain on paper towel and crumble. Drain and dice chilis. Remove and discard the seeds. Chop salmon. Coarsely grate cheeses. Sprinkle all on cooled pie crust.

Place remaining ingredients in blender and mix briefly until well-combined. Pour into crust.

Bake 50-60 minutes at 350° F. (180° C.), or until brown on top and "set." Let stand 5 minutes to cool. Cut in wedges and serve.

Salmon "Coulibiac" Pie

Serves 10 to 12

Easy, delicious Russian pie to serve with melted butter. Can all be made early in day, or two to three hours before serving.

The Crust

4 cups	all-purpose flour, sifted	*1 L*
1 tsp.	salt	*5 mL*
1 cup	butter	*250 mL*
1/2 cup	shortening	*125 mL*
1/2 cup	cold water	*125 mL*

Combine flour and salt in large bowl. Cut in butter and shortening until fine. Add cold water; mix in with fork. Shape into ball and chill a short while. Meanwhile, prepare the filling.

Salmon Filling

	1 medium onion - chopped	
1/4 cup	butter or margarine	75 mL
1/2 lb.	mushrooms - sliced	250 g
1½ lb.	salmon meat without bones or skin	700 g
3/4 cup	dry white wine	200 mL
4 tsp.	dried dillweed	20 mL
1 tsp.	dried leaf tarragon	5 mL
4 cups	cold cooked rice	1 L
4-5 tsp.	salt (to taste)	20-25 mL
1/2 tsp.	pepper	3 mL
	1 egg white - beat until foamy.	
1-2 cups (or more)	(Lots) melted butter and lemon wedges	250 mL - 500 mL

Preparation:

Cook the rice and cool. Saute onion in butter until yellow and tender. Add mushrooms. Cook 3 minutes. Cool.

Poach salmon in wine. Then cool and flake fish. Reserve the cooking liquid. Combine and mix together in large bowl: the cooked onion and mushrooms, the herbs, the cooked rice, 1/2 cup (125 mL) the reserved fish liquid, the salt and pepper.

Roll the chilled dough out onto large floured cloth or dishtowel. Roll dough into rectangle 18" long x 16" wide.
Mound the salmon mixture down center of rectangle, leaving enough space around all edges (about 3-4 inches) to wrap the pastry up and around the filling. Pinch pastry edges together down center of filling and at ends and pat down to seal the seams securely.

Place a long greased, floured cookie sheet face down on the pastry seam. Lift the cloth, and quickly, carefully, invert the pie onto cookie sheet, (ie. turn the whole production upside-down. Requires a firm grip on that towel!). Pastry seam should be face down on cookie sheet with top of pie smooth. Brush pastry with egg white. Cut 3 or 4 vents in top.

If made early in day, chill and then bring to room temperature. Bake 425° F. (220° C.) 50-60 minutes.

Serve with lots of melted butter, (it's a dryish pie), and lemon wedges.

Siwash is our "Ace in the Hole." When the fish aren't biting, when fish aren't *anywhere*, when everyone's gloomy, depressed, bored and, of course, fishless, in desperation we send the troops up to Siwash Bay.

Sure enough, that's often where they're hiding. I can't figure out why all the fish in creation mysteriously mass at Siwash, but, as our last ploy, it's often a winner. Then guests and guides return: tired, victorious, gory. Pressure's off.

Siwash Salmon Steaks

Serves 6

Very easy to make. Basically just baked salmon with sherry, sour cream and dill. A good recipe for boating — fishing trips. Prepare early in day or up to 1 hour before serving.

	6 thick 1 inch (3 cm) large salmon steaks (or 2 lb. / 1 kg)	
1 / 4 cup	flour, or more	75 mL
2 Tbsp.	butter	30 mL
1 / 2 cup	dry sherry (or dry red or white wine — but this is not as good)	125 mL
1 cup	dairy sour cream	250 mL
1 / 2 tsp	dried dillweed	2 mL
1 / 2 cup	minced onion	125 mL
1 / 4 cup	minced green pepper or substitute one 4 oz can *Ortega* mild, green chili peppers — drained, chopped (optional) salt to taste	75 mL

Sprinkle steaks with salt and pepper, roll in flour. Melt butter in large skillet and quickly brown half the steaks on both sides. Place in 9" x 9" pan. Brown remaining 3 steaks in another 2 Tbsp.(30 mL) butter, on both sides. Place in the 9" x 9" pan. Pour skillet butter and juices over. Add sherry.

Heat oven 400⁰F (200⁰C) Bake salmon, covered, 10 minutes. Baste once with its juice.

In a small bowl, mix sour cream, dillweed, onion, green pepper and salt. Stir well.

Remove cover from pan. Spread sour cream mixture evenly over salmon steaks. Sprinkle paprika over top. Bake 15 minutes more at 400⁰F (200⁰C) uncovered until fish flakes and tests "done" with fork in center. Good served with baked, stuffed potatoes (see Vegetables section) or with a rice dish.

Spicy Barbecue Salmon

Serves 8 to 12

Very easy. Tastes like a tender, exotic version of smoked salmon. Has been the consistent favorite of our all-male groups. You could prepare this dish on the beach, on your boat, or even on your apartment balcony. Prepare 6 to 7 hours before you barbecue, since fish needs to marinate. Save all your bacon fat for this.

	8-12 fillets salmon with skin on	
3 cups	Demerara sugar (the coarsest brown sugar)	750 mL
1 cup	coarse or rock salt	250 mL
1 tsp.	nutmeg	5 mL
1 tsp.	cinnamon	5 mL
1 tsp.	garlic powder	5 mL
1/2 tsp.	ground cloves	2 mL
	lots bacon fat	

Slice salmon into fillets, leave skin on. Spread in single layer, skin down, in long, deep pan. In large bowl mix remaining ingredients. Spread evenly over salmon fillets. Gently add enough water to just cover fish. Let stand 5 to 6 hours. Occasionally, stir and spoon sugar mix up over fish. When it's time for the barbecue, light your coals. Drain fish but try to leave fairly thick coating of the sugar glaze on fillets. Melt lots of bacon fat (1/2 cup 125 mL or so). Brush thickly over both sides of fillets. *Slowly* barbecue fillets, meat-side down (facing coals). Remove when slightly undercooked (takes 5 to 10 minutes) and, when ready to serve, finish cooking in hot oven. This saves you fussing over barbecue while guests wait at table!

Japanese Barbecue Salmon Steaks

Serves 4, also good broiled

Excellent to cook on your boat, on shore, or in your back yard.

	4 very thick salmon steaks	
	— at least 1" (3 cm) thick	
1 Tbsp.	cornstarch	15 mL

1 Tbsp.	water	15 mL
5 Tbsp.	dry sherry	75 mL
5 Tbsp.	*Kikkoman* soy sauce	75 mL
2 tsp.	sugar	10 mL

In saucepan, combine cornstarch and water. Add sherry, soy sauce and sugar. Bring to boil. Cool until thick and clear. Cool. Melt 1/4 cup (75 mL) butter, brush fish with some butter, save some for final "topping." Then slather top and sides with one-third of thick sauce. Barbecue or broil on the "sauced" sides 5 to 10 minutes or until half-done. Turn, brush with butter, then spread uncooked tops with one-third more sauce. Cook 5 minutes or until done. Brush remaining butter and sauce over. Serve.

Marco's a small twinkly guy, one of the wittiest guests I know. At mealtimes, he enlivens the table with wisecracks, disaster stories (he broke three ribs on his last visit!), plots to convert the inlet into hamburger stands, or inflammatory pokes at peoples' politics. He connives to convert the lodge into a bawdy-house. Dogmatically, he prods our guides to fish non-existent species. Then, with animation, he fantasizes Daniel Boone-style explorations of the inlet ghost towns.

In reality, Marco's a tough, shrewd lawyer. In the inlet, he's a comic of imaginative contrasts; a noble, though accident-prone, pioneer, a sensitive guy. He approved this recipe, though I don't think he guessed it would bear his name.

Marco's Poached Salmon in Coriander and Wine

Serves 4 to 10

> 4-10 thick, (1½ to 2") large steaks
> or
> two small, thick steaks per person
> fresh or dried leaf coriander *or* fresh or
> dried dillweed *or* fresh fennel leaves
> salt and pepper
> any dry, white wine

Slice a 5 to 10 lb. (3-5 kg) salmon into steaks. Wash well. Carefully cut off skin and fat. Arrange, snugly, in 13" x 9" x 2" pan, or 8" x 8" x 2" pan (depending on number of steaks). Sprinkle coriander, salt and pepper over both sides of steaks. Pour in enough wine to come halfway up sides of steaks. Cover pan with foil. Refrigerate until 1½ hours before serving. Then bring to room temperature (or simply bake, cold, longer, at higher temperature).

Meanwhile, make *hollandaise sauce* (see recipe p. 25). Optional add 1 Tbsp. (15 mL) drained pickled capers to hollandaise. Bake fish at 500 ° F (260° C) or until tests done in middle. Baste once or twice. Drain. Serve immediately with hollandaise sauce.

Resort life hums. Float planes busily drone by to drop new, bewildered city people and boxes of groceries. Nervously, I whip off my apron and rush to welcome them. I'm tense, split between unpacking food, preparing meals and bedrooms, and greeting people. Somehow sad at the loss of former guests for another season. So, to get to know each other I seat everyone around a huge introductory snack of cracked crab and, because our guests are often from Arizona or Los Angeles and are partial to Mexican food, Ceviche. Then there's usually carrot cake in the cookie bowl to help ease us into friendship. Here's our chance to chat, "arrive," absorb each other, and relax.

This recipe came from our very first Nebraska guest, George Cook.

"Ceviche" — Mexican Pickled Salmon

Serves 10 to 12

An appetizer or snack. I usually halve the recipe. Lasts one week in fridge. Prepare 24 hours ahead, since fish must marinate this long.

5-6 lbs	*fresh* salmon fillets	3 kg
8 oz. each	2 bottles *Realime*	220 mL ea
	2 medium onions — sliced thin (into rings)	
	6 bay leaves	
2 cups	white vinegar	500 mL
	30 whole peppercorns	
1/2 tsp	cayenne	2 mL
1½ Tbsp	salt or more to taste	25 mL
2 Tbsp.	sugar to taste	30 mL
1/2 tsp.	*Coleman's* dried mustard powder	2 mL
	handful dried parsley flakes	
2Tbsp.	olive oil	30 mL
	6 whole, dried red chili pods	

Remove skin from fish and cut in strips 2" (4 cm) long, 1/2" (1 cm) thick. Place fish in deep pot with lid, or flat deep roasting pan, and add other ingredients. Stir well. Cover. Chill in fridge 24 hours. Stir occasionally. If ceviche starts to lose its "bite," add more salt. Eat an onion slice with each strip of fish. Piquant taste !

Many Canadian guests welcome foreign or exotic foods —
especially Mexican.

Salmon or Crab Enchiladas

Serves 6
Can be made early in day, chilled in fridge, then brought to
room temperature 1½ hours before serving. Excellent with
steamed greens (broccoli, peas) or with romaine salad and
French bread, or corn chips and guacamole.

Filling

3/4 cup	dairy sour cream	*200 mL*
1½ cups	crabmeat - drained and flaked,	*375 mL*
	or	
	canned salmon	
1/2 tsp.	chili powder	*2 mL*
1/2 tsp.	cayenne	*2 mL*
½-¾ tsp.	salt - or to taste	*2-3 mL*
1 tsp.	ground cumin powder	*5 mL*
1/2 cup	coarsely-grated sharp cheddar	*125 mL*
1/2 cup	chopped scallions (green onions)	*125 mL*

Stir ingredients in medium bowl and chill.

Flour Tortillas

2 cups	all-purpose flour	*500 mL*
1 tsp.	salt	*5 mL*
1/4 cup	shortening	*75 mL*
1/2 cup	lukewarm water	*125 mL*

Stir together flour and salt. Cut in shortening until crumbly. Stir
in water. Knead smooth. Cut and shape into 12 equal balls.
Cover with damp towel. Let stand 20 minutes.

Enchilada Sauce

1 cup	plain tomato sauce (7½ oz. tin)	*250 mL*
1/2 tsp.	dried leaf oregano	*2 mL*
1/2 tsp.	dried leaf basil	*2 mL*
	2 large garlic cloves - crushed	
1/4 tsp.	cayenne	*1 mL*
1/4 tsp.	chili powder	*1 mL*

Combine ingredients in small sauce pan. Heat to boil, stirring, remove from heat. Set to one side.

Garnish

Prepare and reserve:

1 cup	dairy sour cream	250 mL
¼-½ cup	chopped scallions	75-125 mL
1 cup	coarsely-grated sharp cheddar	250 mL

Fry Tortillas:

Heat 8" ungreased iron skillet. Roll one ball of dough into thin 6" to 8" round. Cook on one side in hot skillet until air bubbles rise and freckle light brown. (*Note:* These may not rise until you turn tortilla). Dough should remain white between the brown freckles. Watch carefully not to burn! Turn tortilla with spatula. Cook other side in same manner. Repeat process with remaining balls of dough. Stack cooked tortillas on plate, keeping top layer covered with towel. Warm the enchilada sauce. Lightly brush each tortilla on both sides with the warm sauce. Divide crab or salmon filling into 12 equal portions and spread one portion along bottom third of each tortilla. Roll tortillas up, crepe-fashion, and place in greased 9" x 13" pan. Sprinkle the 1 cup grated cheddar evenly over enchiladas. Cover. Refrigerate until 1 to 1½ hours before baking time. Then bring to room temperature. Bake, uncovered, 375° F (190° C) 20 to 30 minutes or until heated through.

To Serve:
Spread sour cream evenly over cooked, hot enchiladas, and sprinkle with reserved scallions. Serves 2 tortillas per person.

In winter, we tow our resort down Knight Inlet to Heron Cove, a narrow-cliffed enclave protected from northern gales by Bones Bay.

I suppose my warmest memory of Heron Cove is the quality of tranquillity. On those gray, winter mornings, I loved getting up early to light the woodstove. Feet propped on hearth, mug of hot, strong coffee in my lap, I'd nest — waiting for morning.

First came the westerly. Sometimes soft wind-murmur; sometimes roaring wind-waves against Bones Bay's cliffs. Swaying, writhing through twisted trees. The westerly: a sucking graywater hunger against our log wharf. I felt safe. Enclosed and protected by the land. On winter mornings, surrounded by energy, I rested at the calm center. Accepted by Heron Cove.

One winter, I invented this recipe at Heron Cove.

Heron Cove Crab, Chicken or Salmon Chalupas

Serves 4 to 6

This recipe can be doubled, and you may substitute chicken or canned salmon for the crab. Make 3 or 4 hours ahead and impress everyone with your leisurely approach to the meal hour.

Guacamole - Make early in day.

	1 medium tomato	
	2 large, ripe avocados — peeled, pitted, halved,	
1 Tbsp.	fresh lemon juice	15 mL
2 Tbsp.	fine-chopped onion	30 mL
1 Tbsp.	olive oil	15 mL
1/2 tsp.	Tabasco sauce	2 mL
1/2 tsp.	salt	2 mL
1/8 tsp.	white pepper	1 mL

Dip tomato into boiling water until skin crinkles, then peel and halve. Retain pulp, but squeeze out juice and seeds. Place pulp in small bowl. Add avocados and lemon and mash all together, coarsely, with fork. Add remaining ingredients. Stir well. Chill several hours, until serving time. Keep well covered (or it turns gray!)

Tortillas

       4-6 cornmeal tortillas (I buy these)
Fry crisp in 1'' (3 cm) oil. Drain on paper towels. Set to one side.

Garnishes

3-5 cups	lettuce shredded	1 L
	2 hard boiled eggs, sliced	
1 cup	old, sharp cheddar, grated	250 mL
	green onions (any amount), chopped	
	black olives, sliced	

Chill all in separate bowls.

Sour Cream Filling - Combine the following.

1 cup	dairy sour cream	250 mL
1/4 cup	chopped green olives	75 mL
1/4 cup	sliced ripe (black) olives	75 mL
	2 mild, green canned chilis — chopped, drained	
1-2 cups	canned salmon — drained or drained crabmeat or chunks cooked chicken	250-500 mL
1-2 tsp.	ground cumin powder or more to taste	5-10 mL
1-3 tsp.	chili powder to taste	5-15 mL
1/4-1/2 tsp.	cayenne to taste	1-2 mL

    At serving time, arrange all ingredients on large platter in the following order:
- First, the crisp tortillas.
- Then mound lettuce evenly over each tortilla.
- Sprinkle half the cheddar evenly over lettuce.
- Spread the sour cream filling evenly over the cheese.
- Arrange egg slices over the filling.
- Top each tortilla with large dollop guacamole (reserve any left over as dip for corn chips or vegetables or spread for Eggs Benedict).

    Sprinkle remaining cheese, sliced olives and green onions over all.

    Serve

    Messy! You eat using fingers, so have a pile of napkins handy.

In Japan, I was lonely. It was hard to traverse the culture —language differences. So I expressed my experience and perceptions and feelings for that land silently...through cooking. Lots of oriental "wok" dishes. I came up with this tempura recipe.

Now, in the inlet, there's the warmth of communication and people. The Japan experience has lent an edge of appreciation for their presence.

Still, during my often isolated cooking day, when the boats are "off fishing," I sometimes remember that extreme loneliness.

Now I value my peace, and aloneness; knowing that the boats will return.

Prawn or Salmon or Vegetable Tempura

Serves 4 to 6

Marinated thin slices of fish and / or vegetables fried crisp in a lace-thin batter. Can prepare early in day, or 1 hour before cooking. I serve the tempura with soy sauce — for dipping.

Salmon

	4 to 6 salmon fillets	
1/4 cup	dry sherry	*75 mL*
1/4 cup	soy sauce (*Kikkoman* brand is best)	*75 mL*
	1-2 cloves garlic, crushed	

Skin and cut off fat (gray area of flesh) from fish. Slice into long thin strips (e.g., 1/4"/1 cm thick, 2"/5 cm long). Mix remaining ingredients to marinate fish at least 30 minutes. Stir occasionally.

Prawns

2 lb   prawns (or enough for 4 people)

Partially steam prawns in shells until only half done. Pour 1 kg. cold water over to cool. Remove shells — I cut prawn shell up the back with scissors, hold onto tail and pull the meat out with my fingers. Slice prawns lengthwise in half so you have two long, thin, partially-cooked halves. Cover and chill until ready to fry.

Vegetables

> zucchini
> carrots
> broccoli
> cauliflower

Slice into long, very thin strips. Don't peel unless peel tastes bitter or seems tough. Cover and chill until ready to fry.

Tempura Beer Batter

Makes 2 cups but recipe can be halved for smaller amounts of fish or vegetables.

1 2/3 cup	rice flour (health food stores carry this)	425 mL
1½ tsp.	salt	7 mL
1 tsp.	baking powder	5 mL
	3 eggs	
	one 12 oz. bottle beer, unopened	

Sift dry ingredients into medium bowl. Beat eggs until frothy. Open beer. Stir into frothy eggs alternately the flour mixture and the beer. Beat if lumpy. Makes very thin batter.

Heat oil (I prefer safflower oil) until it is very hot. Have plenty of paper towel-covered platters ready to drain tempura.

Dip a few items at a time into batter and quickly drop into pot. Stir up from bottom. Cooks very quickly.

When done, immediately drain on towel and rush to table. Have soy sauce available in saucers for dipping the prawns or vegetables, though salmon should not be dipped since it is marinated in soy sauce. I often add vinegar to the soy dip for a more piquant taste.

Octopus are a nuisance! They crawl into our crab traps to devour the crab, then they're impossible to extract. A mass of slime, suctioned on to the trap mesh. However, octopus *is* delicious to eat. I have a tacit "octopus delivery system" with our neighboring "green boat" camp. We trade their unwelcome intruders for my cookie bowl. Here's my best octopus dish. A Chinese saute that uses one large or two medium octopus.

Octopus Wok

Serves 4 to 6

Prepare octopus early in day. Clean by cutting off all white meat from head area; reserve meat. Cut off tentacles, scraping or cutting off suction cups. Reserve tentacles. Pull off skin using sharp fillet knife - this is the most tedious part, the rest of the recipe is easy. Cut octopus meat (should be all white) into large chunks. You should have 1-2 cups (250-500 mL) meat per person, since it shrinks when cooked.

Sprinkle octopus liberally with commercial powdered tenderizer, and pressure cook or boil until tender (takes 30 minutes in pressure cooker or 2 hours to boil). Test tenderness - chew a piece! Looks awful, but have faith....

Vegetables

garlic cloves and fresh ginger
broccoli
green beans
frozen peas, thawed
celery
cauliflower
onion
or whatever other vegetables you have on hand.

Slice diagonally in thin Chinese style, and reserve in separate containers. Prepare enough to serve 4 to 6 people when sauteed.

Sauce

1-2 cups	chicken stock	*250-500 mL*
2-3 Tbsp.	cornstarch	*30 mL*
	ground coriander - lots, to taste	
1-2 Tbsp.	soy sauce (or more, to taste)	*15-30 mL*

Combine in small bowl. Stir well and set aside.

To Serve: Heat 1/4 cup (75 mL) vegetable oil in large wok and saute 2-4 large crushed garlic cloves and 1-3 slices fresh ginger, crushed or minced. Stir in vegetables, one type at a time. Stir-fry and steam until tender-crisp, remove with slotted spoon, then cook next variety. Don't cook frozen peas!

When all vegetables are cooked combine octopus, vegetables, peas and sauce in wok and heat quickly, stirring. Add salt to taste. Serve immediately, garnished with toasted sesame seed if you like. Good with rice or noodles.

Oriental Fish Cubes
Serves 4 to 6

A good "boating dish"; easy to prepare and quick to cook.

Crispy, fried strips of salmon, cod, or any whitefish. Good with boiled, then fried, oriental noodles mixed with toasted sesame seeds.

Make *at least* two hours before serving, since fish has to marinate.

4 fillets salmon or cod

Cut 1" (3 cm.) thick x 2" (5 cm.) long, in strips.

The Marinade:

2 tsp.	grated onion	*10 mL*
1/4-1/2 tsp.	powdered ginger	*1-2 mL*
1 tsp.	sugar	*5 mL*
2 tsp.	cornstarch	*10 mL*
1/4 cup	dry sherry	*75 mL*
1/4 cup	*Kikkoman* soy sauce	*75 mL*
	1 egg - beaten	
	(optional) 1 clove garlic - crushed	

Mix and stir well. Submerge fish in marinade. Chill at least 2 hours. Stir occasionally.

Fine grind 3/4 cup (175 mL) raw almonds *or* have 3/4 cup (175 mL) fine cornflake, bread, or cracker crumbs (I like the cornflake!). Keep 1/2 cup (125 mL) more crumbs handy, in case you need more than recipe calls for.

Forty minutes before serving roll each marinated fish cube in crumbs to coat well. Stand cubes apart, separated, on pan for 30 minutes. Allow to dry at room temperature.

Then heat 1/4 cup (75mL) safflower oil in large skillet or wok. Saute fish cubes, quickly, over high heat, turning to brown all sides. Add more oil if necessary.

Drain on paper towels and serve immediately.

I proudly named this recipe after myself to honor the 50 lb. (25 kg.) monster cod I caught while jigging for dinner.

Lee's Mandarin Cod or Prawns

For 4   (Recipe can be doubled)

In this recipe, seafood is quickly sauteed and then served in a hot and sweet sauce.

Can make early in day, or two to three hours before serving.

1 lb. or more	prawn meat (equals 2 to 3 lb. prawns in shell)	*500 g*
	or	
1 lb. or more	cod meat	*500 g*
1/2 cup	minced scallions	*125 mL*
1/2 cup	minced zucchini, or combination of celery and/or bean sprouts, or bamboo shoots	*125 mL*
1/4 tsp.	crushed fresh ginger root (I use my garlic press to crush the ginger) 3 large garlic cloves - crushed 1-2 green onions	*1 mL*

Shell at least 2 lb. (1 kg) prawns to end up with 1 lb (500 g) prawn meat, or cut cod into large chunks. Chill. Combine vegetables, ginger and garlic in small bowl and set aside. Slice green onions into large slivers and reserve for garnish.

Sauce

2 Tbsp.	sugar	*30 mL*
1/2 cup	catsup	*125 mL*
3 Tbsp.	sherry	*45 mL*
1 Tbsp.	soy sauce	*15 mL*
1 Tbsp.	toasted sesame seeds (I toast raw sesame)	*15 mL*
1/2 tsp.	Tabasco sauce	*2 mL*

Combine ingredients in small bowl and set aside.
In a cup, mix and set to one side:

1 Tbsp.	cornstarch	*15 mL*
3 Tbsp.	water	*45 mL*

Bring fish to room temperature.
10-20 minutes before serving, heat in deep wok or heavy pot

1 cup (250 mL) oil, (I use safflower or any leftover oil which I reserve, chilled for deep frying). *Barely* deep-fry the seafood until *just* cooked on outside (1-2 minutes), drain and sieve and reserve oil. Place fish or prawns on paper towels to drain. Place 2 Tbsp. (30 mL) of the reserved oil in wok. (Chill the remainder for future frying.) Heat and add the scallion-zucchini mixture. Stir-fry 1 minute. Add seafood and catsup-sherry mixture, then cornstarch-water mixture. Heat quickly to thicken and complete the cooking of the seafood.

Sprinkle sliced green onions over to garnish. Serve immediately.

Calmly, Lull Bay curves out into Knight Inlet on one side, then narrows into a green river valley between the mountains. We nestle near its shore, protected from the ocean and westerly winds.

I love this view from my kitchen windows, especially the evidence of man's presence. On one side, twisted, eroded pilings sag out from the river, remains of a past logging camp. On the other side crouches Hoeya Head - that green hump of land flattening out to a beaver-tail point. This is our fishing ground: daily goal of our red fishing boats. At "The Point" eagles and kelp beds and salmon wait. Waves and winds of the inlet challenge men, boats and fish alike. The sun warms them; the mountains awe them. And, at the end of such a day, I feed them. Dishes such as the following:

Lull Bay Lemon Cod

Serves 6

2 lb.	6 fillets, fresh or frozen cod or sole (also can substitute salmon)	1 kg
1 tsp.	salt	5 mL
	6 sprigs or sprinkles fresh or dried dillweed	
2 cups	water	500 mL
	3 onion slices	
	1 bay leaf	
	2 whole allspice (or 2 liberal pinches of the powder)	
2 tsp.	salt	10 mL
	1 slice unpeeled lemon	

Cut each fillet into 4" (10 cm) lengths. Sprinkle all, liberally, on both sides with salt and dill. Roll fillets up. Fasten each with a toothpick. Combine remaining ingredients in saucepan and simmer, uncovered, 15 minutes. Strain. Place fillets in large skillet, pour liquid over them, cover and simmer 3-5 minutes (until just opaque on outside, but uncooked on inside). Carefully remove fish, (reserve the liquid).

Lemon Sauce

3-4 Tbsp.	butter	45-60 mL
2 Tbsp.	butter	30 mL

1 cup	of the reserved liquid	250 mL
	2 egg yolks, with	
1/2 cup	cream or evaporated milk	125 mL
1 Tbsp.	lemon juice	15 mL
1 Tbsp.	butter	15 mL

Melt butter in saucepan, stir in flour and then reserved liquid. Simmer, uncovered, for a few minutes. In a small bowl, beat eggs and milk. Slowly stir some of the hot sauce into this. Slowly stir all back into remaining hot sauce in saucepan. Cook and stir over *low* heat until smooth and thick. Watch not to curdle with too high a heat! Remove sauce from heat and add lemon juice and remaining butter.

Arrange fish in greased 9"x 9" baking dish. Warm the sauce (don't allow to boil!), reserve and keep warm. Bake fish uncovered, 400° F. (200° C.) for 10-15 minutes or until cooked through. Remove from oven, pour warm sauce over, serve.

I'm convinced there are cod lurking at Stormy Bluff. Except for the powerful current (cod prefer peace and quiet, I hear), Stormy Bluff *looks* ideal: steep cliffs plummeting into deep cold waters. But according to my "cod psychology," cod actually *know* there's no place for us to tie up there, or to anchor while we jig. The water is so strong and deep, we're lucky to even trap prawns. Our cod-jigging's a failure!

It's a bit embarrassing to have such trouble catching cod. Doesn't fit our "fish expert" image. However, since I prefer that delicate white meat to salmon, and guests love the variety of tastes cod is capable of, we work hard to jig them. I'm as happy to catch cod as any Tyee salmon.

Stormy Bluff Fennel Seafood
Cod, Prawns, Clams

Serves 6 to 8

Basically, this dish is steamed seafood, pasta, or vegetables in a herbed tomato sauce. It's simple and quick to do. At most, the sauce takes 20 minutes to prepare. It's complemented by the addition of any mild white cheese, or sharp cheddar or parmesan, as a melted topping. I like the subtle, licorice flavor it imparts to vegetables.

Prepare (cook) your vegetables or pasta or seafood. Choose enough for 6 to 8 people: (e.g. 60 to 80 clams, *or* 2 eggplant, *or* 6 to 8 zucchini, *or* 1½ to 2 lb. cod or shelled prawnmeat). Cook your pasta al dente. Reserve. Zucchini and eggplant are good mixed.

Cut cod or vegetables into large chunks. Steam until partially cooked (vegetables should still be crispy, cod or prawns should be barely cooked through). Salt lightly. Chill. While vegetables or seafood steam, prepare sauce.

The Tomato Sauce

Use the amount you need and chill any leftover sauce for future use.

1 large onion - chopped
4 large cloves garlic - crushed

1/4 cup	parsley	75 mL
1 tsp.	dried leaf basil	5 mL
1/2-1 tsp.	dried leaf tarragon	2-5 mL
1/2 tsp.	whole fennel seeds - crush in palm	2 mL
6 Tbsp.	olive oil	100 mL
	liberal dash cayenne	
28 oz.	one can whole tomatoes, undrained	1 L
1½ tsp.	salt	7 mL
1/2 cup	evaporated milk	125 mL

Heat oil in medium saucepan. Add onion, garlic and seasonings. Saute, briefly, until onion transparent and yellow. Add cayenne. Add tomatoes and mash tomatoes into sauce with fork. Simmer, uncovered until reduced and thick (40 minutes or more). Remove from heat and add salt and milk. Set aside to cool.

When sauce is cool, arrange the pasta or vegetables or seafood in 8" x 8" baking dish. (Optional) - layer shredded cheese (Monterey Jack, or Swiss, or Cheddar, with some Parmesan) through the vegetables or seafood or pasta, for a lasagne-style dish. You might need to salt the layers. Spoon lots sauce over and stir to sink down through the layers. Sprinkle cheese over top.

Pre-heat oven 350° F. (180° C.). Heat dish 10 to 20 minutes, until cheese melted and vegetables or seafoods are hot through. Serve immediately.

The Georgie, in her worst moments, is an orange pig. I say this with nostalgic affection - that she's our power speedboat is irrelevant.

At "The Point," *Georgie* loves wallowing in weedy kelp beds. She's a stubborn hell to untangle and clean off. Snout down, she gruntingly plows through the waves, cheerfully gassing guests at her rear while nauseating those at her bow. People (qu)easily feel seasick in these rough, pounding waters, and there's no way *Georgie* is light or delicate on her keel.

Despite her porcine appearance and movements, however, *Georgie* is our lifeline in the wilderness. Without her, we'd be totally cut off from the world. She houses our radio-phone (our communication, here). She transports our guests to the fishing grounds. In springtime she transforms into the resort's moving van, lugging all our new gear, outboards, and guides. With dogged loyalty she fetches our mail from Minstrel Island.

Years ago, *Georgie* was our bedroom. Since our first lodge was too small to accommodate us, I spent those summer nights retiring to the moldy boudoir of *Georgie*. Unromantically, I slept over the toilet. Uneasily, I slept to the sloshing waves beneath my ear. On stormy nights you might say I was rocked, violently, to sleep.

We named our speedboat after my sister, *Georgie:* She loved this prawn recipe.

Georgie's Prawn Stroganoff

Serves 4

(Great with saffron rice and artichokes, or with toasted poppy or sesame seeds in the rice). Make ahead, (it takes 30 minutes to prepare), then re-heat at serving time.

1/4 cup	minced onion	*75 mL*
3 Tbsp.	butter or margarine	*45 mL*
1½ lb.	shelled prawnmeat (equals about	*750 g*
	3 lb. prawns in shell)	*1½ kg*
1/2 lb.	mushrooms - halved	*250 g*
1 Tbsp.	butter	*15 mL*
1 Tbsp.	flour or more (to 2 Tbsp.)	*15 mL*
1¼ tsp.	salt	*6 mL*
	pepper to taste	
1½ cups	dairy sour cream	*375 mL*

Melt butter in large skillet and saute onion. Add prawns and saute 3 minutes or until opaque and barely pink, removing smaller prawns first, as they tend to cook quicker. Remove prawns with slotted spoon and set to one side in a dish. Leave prawn juice in skillet. Add mushrooms and remaining butter. Saute until mushrooms barely cooked. Sprinkle in flour, stir, remove from heat, stir in the prawns, sour cream, salt and pepper. Re-heat and serve.

If you prepare ahead, remember to re-heat for only 5 to 10 minutes. Don't allow to boil, and watch not to overcook! Prawns easily turn to mush!

Meats

Every night at 5:30 the boats return, guests hungry and ready for my big dinner. I rush to turn off the generator so that we can eat in peace, at one with the beauty of Lull Bay. Companionship, warmth, laughter, drinks, a time of gathering after confronting the vast silence of the inlet. Appetites are enormous!

Then, at 7 p.m., they're off! Out for the evening fish! My generator and dishwasher roar to life. I clean up and prepare the "6 a.m. snack" for next morning. Finally, I make my breads and leave the dough to rise while I settle down for a quick cup of tea before our boats return.

Resort dinners are a blend of exotic dishes and everyone's favorites. Using foreign countries and regional flavor for inspiration, I like to evoke a certain character or theme.

As you read this section you'll notice the influence: French-Canadian, traditional English and American, French, Swiss, Italian and Greek. For me, it's fun to explore diverse cultures through food.

The old wood hotel on Minstrel Island has been operating for fifty years now. On chilly winter evenings, local people gather in the parlor-pub to chat, play crib or cards, pass time in a slow, relaxing way. Some drift to shelves of borrowable books. Others lazily warm their hands over the wheezy oil heater at the back. At times the aged inn resounds to energetic fifties-style rock dance; or to spontaneous dinners: the sharing of a recent prawn-catch, or pot of crab.

In summer, yachting tourists uncertainly Bermuda-short their way through the inn's dark halls. Local families sun on its rickety steps. Sparkling, zesty, and tasting of salmon barbecues new life flows past the hotel.

For me, Swallow Inn's green-lawn, flower-gardened cultivation holds charm: a mellow-aging in the tempestuous inlet.
One moonlit night we boated this pie over to Swallow Inn for a community feast.

"Swallow Inn" Steak And Kidney Pie

Serves 8 to 10

This recipe is hearty, filling and uses an interesting combination of wine and herbs to catch your taste. You'll need a large 5-quart casserole (preferably cast iron) to bake it in. Leave yourself plenty of time - this takes about 2 hours to prepare.

	5-8 slices bacon	
2 lb.	beef kidneys	1 kg
3 lb.	stewing beef	1.5 kg
1 cup	dry, red wine	250 mL
	3 medium carrots, cut into chunks	
	2 potatoes, diced	
1½ cups	onions, thinly sliced	375 mL
1/2 lb.	mushrooms, sliced	500 g

Gravy

1 cup	reserved wine juice	250 mL
1/2 cup	flour	125 mL
1 cup	dry, red wine	250 mL
1 Tbsp.	salt	15 mL
3/4 tsp.	pepper	3 mL
1 tsp.	dried leaf thyme	5 mL
1/4 tsp.	dried sage powder	1 mL
1 Tbsp.	tomato paste	15 mL

Chop bacon and fry until crisp. Drain on paper towel. Retain 1 Tbsp. (15 mL) drippings in skillet and fry diced kidneys just until loses pinkness on outside.

Cut beef into 2''x 2'' (5 cm x 5 cm) chunks, sprinkle liberally with meat tenderizer, and cook 10 minutes in wine in pressure cooker.

You may *boil* it in 2 cups (500 mL) wine, but this takes 2 hours so start early! I often make the crust (see recipe for Aunt Dot's Butter Pastry on page 132 double it for this pie) at this point, while meat cooks.

Strain meat. Reserve juice. Add a little juice to pressure cooker with carrots and potatoes. Pressure cook 1 minute *or* steam until just tender. Reserve juice. Add cooked vegetables to meat in large bowl, then add onions, mushrooms and bacon. Mix.

In a saucepan, combine flour with 1/2 cup (125 mL) of the reserved meat liquid, stirring to a smooth paste. Stir in further 1/2 cup (125 mL) reserved liquid, (use the liquid from the vegetables if necessary), and wine. Add seasonings and tomato paste. Boil until very thick.

Gently fold gravy into meat and vegetable mix in bowl. Stir to coat all pieces. Place in greased deep 5-quart casserole.

Roll out the double crust to thickly cover the casserole ingredients. Scallop the edges with fingers. Cut 3 vents in middle.

Pre-heat oven to 425° F. (220° C.). Beat one egg to frothy. Brush evenly over crust. Bake pie, uncovered, 50 minutes, or until crust nicely browned. Place on rack to cool and 'set' 10 minutes. Serve, making sure you dig deep to bottom of pot for all the goodies.

My French-Canadian sister-in-law, Viv, introduced me to the subtleties of herb and spice use, and a more continental or gourmet approach to cookery. Many of my "dog-eared," well-used and loved recipes came from Viv's files.

With Viv, I learned how to instinctively balance courses and dishes in a meal: hot and cold foods, heavy and light foods, texture-blends and nutrition. To accompany her tourtiere, for instance, I recommend you balance the meal with a crunchy green salad, such as Spencer's Simple Romaine, p 48, for the first course; then a light, steamed vegetable to complement the heavy pie. Finish up with a cold, fluffy dessert, perhaps Wine-Berry Meringue, p.140, or a mousse of your choice, or Strawberry Fluff, p.133. Strawberries Jubilee p.135. Would be good, too.

Viv's Tourtiere

Serves 6 to 8

A heavy, filling, French-Canadian meat pie. Viv traditionally concocts this for Christmas. It can be frozen then thawed and baked.

Double recipe of Aunt Dot's Butter Pastry, see p. 132 or use Salmon Coulibiac crust recipe p. 86.

1 lb.	ground pork	500 g
1/2 lb.	hamburger, (or	250 g
	1½ lb if you can't get pork)	
	2 celery stalks and leaves	
	- fine-chopped	
	1 or 2 medium onions - fine-chopped	
	1 large carrot - grated	
	(I use Cuisinart for those three items.)	
1 tsp.	cinnamon	5 mL
1/2 tsp.	dried leaf summer savory	2 mL
	- crush in palm	
2 tsp.	salt	10 mL
1/4 tsp.	pepper	1 mL
	1 bay leaf	
	1 large garlic clove - crushed	
1 cup	boiling water	250 mL
1½-2 Tbsp.	flour	20-30 mL
	1 egg yolk	

First prepare and pre-bake the pastry. Divide pastry in two halves. Roll out enough of one half to fit 9" or 9½" pie plate. Prick all over with fork, bake 400° F. (220° C.), 10 to 15 minutes, or until partly baked but still white. Cool on rack.

Meanwhile, roll out enough of the remaining pastry half to fit pie plate. Place on plate. Cover and chill until ready to fit on top of pie. Chill any leftover pastry to use for tarts or turnovers.

Place meat, vegetables and seasonings in large iron saucepan, add boiling water. Cover. Simmer 45 minutes, low heat, then stir in flour to thicken (should resemble a thick mush!). Cool thoroughly (refrigerate).

When filling is cool, pour it into baked and cooled pie shell. Place top crust over. Scallop edges with fingers to seal. Cut three slits in top. Brush pie with 1 egg yolk, beaten.

Bake, 400° F. (200° C.) 45 minutes. Then let stand on rack 10 minutes, to cool and "set." Serve.

113

Coast people get easily bored with seafood. It's *always* available: down at local wharves, through fishing families or friends, in your backyard coves, or even in city fish markets where seiners drop the fish off, fresh.

So, for guests who are used to coast life, I concentrate on interesting meat dishes. Well-spiced, wine-flavored Italian foods are especially popular.

Lee's Lasagne

Serves 8 to 10

True, *everyone* has a lasagne recipe. However, here's my favorite, well-tested version. Our male groups particularly like it. Serve with Greek salad and French bread.

Meat Sauce

	2 slices cut-up bacon	
1/4 cup	olive oil	75 mL
	5 large cloves garlic - crushed (use your garlic press)	
	1 large onion - chopped	
2 Tbsp.	fine-chopped carrot	30 mL
2 Tbsp.	fine-chopped celery	30 mL
1½ lb.	hamburger	750 g
1/2 lb.	salami or any similar sausage or wieners - chopped	250 g
1/2 tsp.	powdered allspice	2 mL
1 tsp.	dried leaf marjoram	5 mL
1/4 cup	chopped parsley	75 mL
2½ tsp.	powdered oregano	12 mL
19 oz.	one can tomatoes, undrained - cut them up in pot.	540 mL
12 oz.	one can tomato paste	343 mL
1/2 cup	dry red wine	125 mL
1 Tbsp.	salt	30 mL
1/4 tsp.	pepper	1 mL

| 12 oz. | broad lasagne noodles (equals 12 to 14 noodles) | 350 g |
| 12 oz. or more | Mozzarella or Monterey Jack cheese | 350 g |

Fry bacon until crisp. Add oil, onion, garlic, celery and carrot and cook briefly until soft. Stir in seasonings and meat, cook until browned, then add tomatoes, tomato paste, wine, salt and pepper.

Simmer, uncovered, 45 minutes or until very thick. Meanwhile, cook noodles to "al dente." Rinse in cold water and keep covered in cold water until ready to use (keeps them from sticking!). Prepare:

Cream Sauce

1/4 cup	flour	75 mL
2 cups	milk	500 mL
1/2 cup	parmesan	125 mL
	1 egg, beaten	
1/2 tsp.	salt	2 mL
1/4 tsp.	pepper	1 mL

In medium saucepan, make a paste from flour and milk. Add milk slowly until mixture is well-blended, then heat and boil, stirring, until thick. Add Parmesan, egg, salt and pepper. Reheat, stirring, to hot. Set aside. Should be very thick sauce.

Chop or grate Mozzarella or Monterery Jack cheese.

Grease 13"x 9"x 2" baking pan. Spread thin layer of tomato sauce on bottom of pan. Place layer of noodles (3-4) over sauce. Layer cream sauce thinly over noodles. Sprinkle one-quarter of the chopped Mozzarella over cream sauce. Repeat layers in this order, saving some tomato sauce and Mozzarella as final topping.

Bake lasagne 40 minutes at 375° F. (190° C.), or until bubbling and browned on top. Remove from oven and let 'set', cooling, for 10 minutes on rack. Cut into squares. Serve.

Periodically John and our guides tire of exotic foods or fish. They want hamburgers or stew or steak. Above all they crave pizza.

This is one they like.

Northern Pizza

Serves 8 to 16

(Recipe can be halved for 4 to 8 servings.) This recipe makes two huge 12" (30 cm) pizzas. They're cheesy, thick with tomato sauce and herbs; crunchy crust on the bottom. For only one pizza, make whole recipe of the crust and save half for next time.

The Crust

1 pkg.		
(1 Tbsp.)	*Fleischmann's* active dry yeast	15 mL
1½ cup	warm water	375 mL
3-4 cups	all-purpose flour	750 mL
		-1 L
2 tsp.	salt	10 mL

In large bowl, dissolve yeast in 1/2 cup (125 mL) water. Let it stand 5 minutes, then stir. Beat in 1 cup (250 mL) flour and salt, and 1/2 cup (125 mL) water. Add 1 more cup (250 mL) flour. Beat again. Stir in final 1/2 cup (125 mL) water and 1-2 cups (250-500 mL) of remaining flour.

Knead dough until well-blended and elastic. Place in large, oiled bowl. Oil top of dough. Let rise at room temperature for 1 to 1½ hours or until doubled. Or rise in fridge at least 2 hours or all day, until 1½ hours before serving. While dough rises, prepare:

Tomato Sauce

	2 onions	
1/4 cup	olive oil	75 mL
1 lb.	hamburger	500 g
	4 cloves garlic, - crushed	
12 oz.	one can tomato paste	338 mL
28 oz.	one can undrained whole tomatoes	1 L
2 tsp.	salt	10 mL
1 Tbsp.	dried leaf oregano	15 mL
1/2 tsp.	dried leaf basil	2 mL
1/2 tsp.	dried leaf thyme	2 mL
1/2 tsp.	dried red pepper pods (chilies)- crushed	2 mL
1 tsp.	dried parsley flakes	5 mL

Heat oil in large iron skillet or pot, brown meat then add onions and garlic. When onions are soft, add remaining ingredients. Cook, covered, 1 hour, or until thick. Stir occasionally. Then set aside until final preparation. While sauce cooks, prepare your pizza toppings.

The Toppings - Make optional combinations of the following:

green peppers and onions - chopped or sliced
pepperoni or salami - sliced into rounds
black or green olives - sliced and drained
mushrooms - sliced thick; partially fried
anchovies - or any other "toppers" you wish
1 lb. (500 g) Mozzarella or Jack cheese *or* combination of white and cheddar cheeses *or* white cheese and parmesan -sliced or grated.

1½ hours before serving, punch down dough. Divide in half. For two pizzas roll each half into a 12" (30 cm) round. For one pizza roll out only one of the halves; reserve remaining dough (wrap well) in fridge for another "pizza day." Place each round on separate long, greased cookie sheets; pinch edges up into rims. Brush dough with oil. Let rest at room temperature 30 minutes. Then pour tomato sauce over the two oiled crusts. Spread to rims. Arrange cheese slices over sauce. Top with optional assorted goodies.Or place cheese over your toppings, if you prefer.

Bake pizzas at 425° F. (220° C.) for 25 minutes or until crust crisp, golden. Cut in wedges (not too easy - crust is very crunchy). Serve!

Wine—Herb Glaze for Roast Turkey

Use this glaze to baste the turkey. It's rich, herby; adds depth to the gravy drippings.

1 cup	butter or margarine	250 mL
	5 or 6 dashes Worcestershire sauce	
1/2 tsp.	crushed dried leaf rosemary	2 mL
1 tsp.	dry mustard powder	5 mL
1/2 tsp.	crushed dried leaf thyme	2 mL
1/2 tsp.	crushed dried leaf tarragon	2 mL
	grated rind of 1 lemon	
1/4-1/2 cup	dry white wine (to your taste!)	75-125 mL

Melt butter and add remaining ingredients. Mix well. Brush glaze over bird. Cover bird with foil. Roast. Baste bird with rest of butter-mix during last 2 hours of roasting (roast it uncovered for the last 2 hours).

Sage And Applenut Stuffing For Roast Turkey Or Chicken

Stuffs 10 to 15 lb. (5-8 kg) bird. Halve recipe for 6 lb. (3 kg) roast chicken. Make up to one hour before you roast bird. Ellen (p. 23) asked for this recipe. In fact I notice that midwestern people especially like it. Perhaps it reminds them of their New England heritage.

8 cups	coarse-grated, then dried, breadcrumbs, (I leave them in oven overnight to dry.)	2 L
1/2 cup	finely chopped walnuts	125 mL
3/4 cup	margarine or butter	225 mL
1 cup	chopped onion	250 mL
	1½ apples - unpeeled and diced	
1/4 cup	celery - diced	75 mL
1/4 cup	chopped parsley	75 mL
1/2 tsp.	dried leaf thyme	2 mL
1½ tsp.	dried leaf sage - crushed	7 mL
1/2 tsp.	poultry seasoning (powder)	2 mL
1/4 tsp.	pepper	1 mL
2 tsp.	salt	10 mL

Melt 1/4 cup (75 mL) margarine, saute onion, apple and celery. Cook until soft, stirring. Add seasonings. When apple mix soft, remove from heat. Toss in breadcrumbs and walnuts. Melt remaining 1/2 cup margarine and add to mixture. Toss well.

Will used to have two rotund, hairy little porkers named Ivan and Boris. Since they were actually wild Bavarian boars, he felt Russian was only appropriate, but when his happy pig family grew, he ran out of Russian names for them.

Freely, Will's pigs roamed and romped around his island. Before long, bewildered visitors found themselves greeted by voraciously friendly herds with a consuming interest in chewing shoes and pant legs. Will would then bellow at them in Russian, or bang their snouts. His boars would beat a quick retreat, but only to plot their next maneuver. Then we'd spot them — gleefully feasting on Beth's sacred garden!

Finally, Will had to reluctantly reduce their population, so he got a chance to try out this recipe in his Freshwater Bay cabin.

Freshwater Bay Glazed Boar or Pork or Spareribs

1/4 cup	soy sauce	75 mL
3 Tbsp.	catsup	45 mL
3 Tbsp.	honey	45 mL
	2 garlic cloves, crushed	
1/4 tsp.	ginger powder	2 mL
	toasted sesame seeds	

Combine in a bowl. Prepare meat by rubbing with tenderizer, then with salt, rosemary or summer savory. Bake, barbecue or fry, basting with the glaze during the last 30 minutes of cooking. If frying, baste with glaze just before serving.

Reserve some glaze to pour over meat at serving time.

One day, while innocently boating, John met a deer. A swimming deer. Politely, John informed the deer it was heading in the wrong direction and he pointed back toward Lull Bay. The deer ignored him, its dark eyes fixed towards the ocean. John circled the deer. He reminded it of its obligations to family and the deer population (we are a bit short on deer here). Hoping to boost its self-esteem, he praised the deer's beauty and swimming style. That strengthened the deer - it dog-paddled toward Japan! Finally in desperation, John lassoed the deer. It would be more soulful to say that John happily led the deer home, but I must confess it eventually ended up in our freezer. That summer we dedicated many resort meals to John's deer and this is one of them. It is derived from Boeuf Bourguignonne, a well-known French stew.

John Reid's Venison Stew

Serves 10

	8-12 slices bacon	
4 lb.	venison (or stewing beef)	2 kg
2 Tbsp.	brandy	30 mL
10 oz. ea.	3 cans consomme or	284 mL
	beef bouillon soup	each
	2 bay leaves	
2 Tbsp.	chopped parsley	30 mL
	2 medium onions, each cut into	
	segments of 8	
1 tsp.	salt - or to taste	5 mL
1/8 tsp.	pepper	1 mL
1 tsp.	dried leaf thyme	5 mL
	4 carrots	
1½ cups	dry red wine	375 mL
1½-2 lb.	mushrooms	about 1 kg
3 Tbsp.	butter, plus	45 mL
1/2 cup	butter	plus 125 mL
3/4 cup	flour	200 mL

Brown bacon, drain, crumble and reserve. In the drippings, brown the meat which has been cut into large chunks. In small saucepan, warm brandy, ignite and pour over meat. Stir and allow flames to go out. Chop onions and carrots and add to meat. Stir in soup, seasonings and wine. Cover and simmer 1½ to 2 hours or until tender. Add more wine if you wish.

Saute mushrooms in 3 Tbsp. (45 mL) butter and reserve.

In small saucepan (use the one you warmed the brandy in) make a roux by melting 1/2 cup (125 mL) butter and stirring in flour until light brown. Slowly add to meat, stirring in just a little at a time so that it won't lump. Then boil stew until it thickens. Add mushrooms and bacon. Serve.

Have lots of hot rye or corn bread ready to sop up the gravy (not exactly French, this, but people love it).

Herb Glaze For
Roast Lamb, Pork Or Venison

Makes enough to cover a 3-5 lb. (2-3 kg) roast. Double recipe for larger roasts.

	1 large clove garlic, crushed	
1 tsp.	salt	*5 mL*
2 tsp.	coarse-ground pepper	*10 mL*
1/2 tsp.	ginger powder	*2 mL*
	1 bay leaf, well crumbled	
1/2 tsp.	dried leaf thyme	*2 mL*
1/2 tsp.	dried leaf sage	*2 mL*
1/2 tsp.	dried leaf rosemary or	*2 mL*
	summer savory or marjoram	
1 Tbsp.	soy sauce	*15 mL*
1 Tbsp.	vegetable oil	*15 mL*

For venison, you may first need to rub the meat with tenderizer or marinate it in wine unless it is very tender.

Cut shallow slits all over roast. Combine glaze ingredients in bowl, stir thoroughly and spoon over meat, rubbing into all sides with hands. Roast meat on a rack over oven pan, basting with juices. Meat done this way is delicious with Ratatouille or Broiled Eggplant (see Vegetables section).

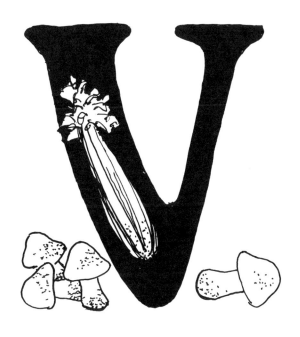

Cooked Vegetable Dishes

My personal bias in the resort is for fresh raw vegetables in salads. When I found to my surprise that lettuces outlived broccoli in my World War II vintage fridge, I was delighted to concentrate on salads. However, for variety I indulge in cooked vegetables at the beginning of every ten-day plane delivery. Then my kitchen blossoms with zucchini and eggplant creations, and with some of the recipes included in this section.

Guests love our wharfed-in hot tub. They return from fishing chilled through, shuck off their wet clothing, concoct a quick drink, and rush past in intriguingly varied underwear, enroute to the hot tub. There they soak, seep, soothe out all the tensions; all the cold; all the responsibilities. Weightless, they float, suspended between ocean and sky. I watch their heads bob from my kitchen windows.

Ollie the otter slithers past enroute to *his* private tub: our bait bucket. Conversation and laughter drift; my cooking tempo harmonizes. When they emerge, I have a hot filling dish waiting.

Stuffed spuds

Serves 5 to 8

This is a gourmet version of Baked Potatoes, especially good with fish dishes. Try it with Marco's Poached Salmon (recipe page 92) or Sherry Salmon Steaks (recipe page 89). I often add some smoked salmon to the filling.

	5 medium baking potatoes	
3 oz	softened cream cheese	200 g
1/2 cup	dairy sour cream	125 mL
2 Tbsp.	whole or canned milk	30 mL
2 Tbsp.	soft butter	30 mL
1 tsp.	onion salt	5 mL
1/2 tsp.	garlic salt	2 mL
1/8 tsp.	white pepper	1 mL
2 Tbsp.	chopped tinned pimento, drained	30 mL
	green onion, chopped parsley,	
	chopped bacon bits or handful	
	chopped smoked salmon — optional	
	salt - to taste	

Wash and prick potatoes and bake 375^{0}F (190^{0}C) for 60-80 minutes until tender. Meanwhile in large bowl, combine cheese, sour cream, milk, butter, salt and pepper. When potatoes are tender, cut large oval flap of skin from top of each and carefully, using teaspoon, scoop out the insides into the cheese mixture. Beat with electric mixer until completely smooth, then stir in remaining seasonings. Add plain salt to taste. Re-fill the hollow potato shells mounding fluffy filling high. Sprinkle with paprika and arrange in pie plate. Bake 30 minutes or more until they test hot in the center.

For 8 people, I use 8 potatoes and increase the recipe by half.

Fennel Vegetables

Serves 6 to 8

Basically, this dish is steamed pasta, or vegetables in a herbed tomato sauce. It's simple and quick to do. At most, the sauce takes 20 minutes to prepare. It's complemented by the addition of any mild white cheese, or sharp cheddar or parmesan, as a melted topping. I like the subtle, licorice flavor it imparts to vegetables. A seafood variation can be found on page 106 .

Prepare (cook) your vegetables or pasta. Choose enough for 6 to 8 people: (e.g.) 2 eggplants, or 6 to 8 zucchini or combine them — 1-2 eggplant to 4 zucchini.)Cook your pasta al dente. Reserve.

Cut vegetables into large chunks. Steam until partially cooked (vegetables should still be crispy through). Salt lightly. Chill. While vegetables steam, prepare sauce.

The Tomato Sauce

Use the amount you need and chill any leftover sauce for future use.

	1 large onion — chopped	
	4 large cloves garlic — crushed	
	liberal dash cayenne	
1/4 cup	chopped parsley	75 mL
1 tsp.	dried leaf basil	5 mL
1/2-1 tsp.	dried leaf tarragon	25 mL
1/2 tsp.	whole fennel seeds — crush in palm	2 mL
6 Tbsp.	olive oil	100 mL
28 oz	can whole tomatoes, undrained	1 L
1 ½ tsp.	salt	7 mL
1/2 cup	evaporated milk	125 mL

Heat oil in medium saucepan. Add onion, garlic and seasonings. Saute, briefly until onion transparent and yellow. Add tomatoes and mash tomatoes into sauce with fork. Simmer, uncovered, until reduced and thick (40 minutes or more). Remove from heat and add salt and milk. Set aside to cool.

When sauce is cool, arrange the pasta or vegetables in 8"x 8" baking dish. (Optional) — layer shredded cheese (Monterey

Jack, or Swiss, or cheddar, with some parmesan) through the vegetables or pasta, for a lasagne-style dish. You might need to salt the layers. Spoon lots sauce over and stir to sink down through the layers. Sprinkle cheese over top.

30 to 40 minutes before serving, pre-heat oven to 350°F. Heat dish 350°F (180°C) 10 to 20 minutes until cheese melted and vegetables are hot through. Serve immediately.

"Changeovers Days" are Hell! At 5 a.m., I reluctantly make up the beds for a new incoming group of guests, then rush to fix breakfast, and start the laundry, housework, and dinner before our seaplane arrives.

It's pressure and it's not easy. Rebellious, sleepy guests get unpolitely kicked out of their nests.... *forced* to go fishing.

Against some resistance, I deluge them with avalanches of clean sheets, vacuum them from their rooms, sweep them into the boats. If that's not enough, I whirl and roar my vacuum at laggards, hammer and shake all doors or feet within reach and flurry unpeacefully about, expertly destroying Lull Bay's quiet.

I'm **not** a delightful presence on changeover days.

Here's a very quick vegetable side-dish, or main meal, to prepare on **your** rushed days.

Scalloped Spinach

Serves 4

A cheesy spinach custard. Serve as a vegetable side-dish or as a vegetarian main course. Can double or triple for more people.

12 oz	1 package frozen spinach	340 g
2 Tbsp.	melted butter	30 mL
	3 eggs, beaten	
2 cups	small curd cottage cheese	500 mL
1 cup	sharp cheddar cheese	250 mL
3/4 tsp.	salt	3 mL
	pepper to taste	
1/8 tsp.	dried dillweed	1 mL
	liberal dash nutmeg	

Thaw spinach, drain well and chop. Add to medium bowl with butter, eggs, cottage cheese and seasonings and mix well. Pour into greased 1 quart casserole or 8 x 8 pan. Bake uncovered 1 hour at 350° F (180° C) or until "set." Serve immediately.

Whenever I prepare ratatouille, I remember hot afternoons in Athens; crowded outdoor vegetable stalls laden with ripe eggplant and zucchini; me returning from my street shopping forays to cook ratatouille over a one-burner hotplate, before rushing down the hill to teach my language classes. Then later, our 10 p.m. Mediterranean-style dinner, with my ratatouille well steeped in its Greek herbs.

Ratatouille: Eggplant and Zucchini Stew

Serves 6 to 8 or more

In the resort, I often serve this with roast lamb, beef or chicken. I concoct this stew by eye, taste and intuition. Here's an approximation. Prepare it early in the day or at least 2 hours before serving so the herbs have time to blend.

1/4 cup	olive oil	75 mL
	4 large cloves garlic - crushed (use your garlic press)	
	1 large onion - chopped	
	2 medium green peppers - chopped large chunks	
	2 chicken bouillon cubes	
	1½-2 eggplant unpeeled - cut in large chunks	
	5-6 medium (6") zucchini (peeled if the skins are bitter) - cut in large chunks	
14 oz	one can whole tomatoes - undrained	398 mL
5½ oz	one can tomato paste	156 mL
	bay leaf	
1/2 tsp.	dried leaf thyme	2 mL
2 tsp.	dried leaf oregano or basil	10 mL
1 Tbsp.	brown sugar	15 mL
	lots of chopped parsley	

Heat oil in large heavy pot. Saute until slightly soft the garlic, onion and green pepper. Add bouillon cubes. Stir in eggplant and zucchini and saute until surfaces slightly cooked but vegetables *very* crisp. Add more oil if necessary. Watch closely since zucchini turns to mush quickly. Remove any softening vegetables and reserve. Add tomatoes, breaking up with spoon. Add thyme, bay leaf, oregano and tomato paste. Cover and simmer, stirring occasionally until vegetables tender-crisp.

127

Stew should form a rich and herby sauce. When cooked, set to one side, adding any vegetables you removed earlier.

To serve: Add salt to taste — probably 1½ - 2 tsp. (8-10 mL). Stir in brown sugar and parsley, re-heat quickly and serve hot. Good as a cold snack, too.

Spinach or Broccoli Quiche

Serves 4 to 8

This quiche is light and quick to prepare, good for brunch, lunch or dinner. It is also delicious using fresh fennel. It comes from the kitchen of a Swiss friend and artist, Ruth.

	9" unbaked pie shell	
1 lb.	fresh broccoli florets, or spinach or	1/2 kg
	or	
10 oz ea.	one-two packages fennel or frozen	280 g
each	spinach	each
	1 large onion - chopped	
1 cup	milk	250 mL
	2 eggs	
1 Tbsp.	flour	15 mL
1 tsp.	salt	5 mL
1/8 tsp.	nutmeg	1 mL
	pepper to taste	
	liberal pinch dried fennel seed	
¼ - ¾ tsp.	fines herbes (a commercial blend)	2-3 mL
1-2 cups	Swiss cheese — optional	200-500 mL

Bake pie shell 10 minutes at 425° F (220° C). Set aside. Steam or boil vegetables to tender. Drain well. Chop and reserve. Fry bacon until crisp, drain and crumble. In bacon fat, saute chopped onion and add with broccoli and bacon to pie shell. Sprinkle cheese over if desired.

Beat milk, eggs, flour and seasonings together. Pour into cooked pie shell to cover the vegetables. Bake a further 20-35 minutes or until it tests "done" in the middle and is golden brown. Serve in wedges.

There are some miserable stormy nights when not *one* guest will go fishing. Even John can't persuade them out into cold howling winds or pounding waves. People simply want to sit around the alder table playing cards, or watching the storms pass, safe behind mugs of hot rum. Eventually, John gives up, climbs out of his raingear and joins them by the woodstove. Then the fishing stories begin... And I perk up my ears to catch the occasional mention of a good recipe, like this one, contributed by Charley and Virginia from Washington State.

Virginia's Stuffed Beets

        whole beets, two per person
        sharp cheddar, grated
        fine breadcrumbs
        salt and pepper to taste
        dried dillweed (optional)
        Parmesan

Steam or boil beets until done. Cool and peel. With teaspoon, scoop out centers of beets, reserving the shells. Mash beet pulp, mix with cheese, breadcrumbs and seasonings to taste. Carefully pack mixture back into beet shells, mounding tops. Place in pie plate or pan. Sprinkle with Parmesan cheese and bake 350° F (180° C) for 20 to 30 minutes or until hot through.

Broiled Eggplant

The taste of eggplant reminds me of fresh bread and mussels. A bland yet tantalising tang to it. Blends beautifully with oregano. Crisps up in spots when broiled. Good accompaniment to seafood dishes, or served with lamb or pork.

1 to 2 large unpeeled eggplant. Leaf oregano or basil (fresh or dried), olive oil. Slice eggplant into 1/4 inch thick slices.

Arrange slices on cookie sheet and brush each slice liberally with olive oil (Greek oil is best). Have more oil at hand to brush bottom sides of eggplant later. Arrange slices, oiled sides facing heat, on broiler pan. Sprinkle dried leaf oregano, or basil, over each slice. Salt slices lightly. Broil until slices turn golden brown (5 minutes or longer). Turn slices, brush tips of slices with oil; sprinkle oregano. Taste and sprinkle more salt if necessary. Broil till eggplant tests tender with fork and is golden brown. Serve immediately.

Spinach or Broccoli Stuffed Tomatoes

Serves 12

A colorful blend of red and green vegetables, mushrooms, sour cream and cheeses. Try serving this dish for lunch for 6 people, using 6 immense tomatoes, or as a dinner vegetable for 12.

	12 medium tomatoes	
10 oz. ea.	2 packages frozen spinach or broccoli	*280 g each*
1/2 lb	fresh sliced mushrooms	*250 g*
1½ cups	mild white cheese (Monterey Jack or Swiss)	*375 mL*
	2 eggs	
1/2 cup	Parmesan cheese	*125 mL*
1 cup	dairy sour cream	*250 mL*
2 tsp.	salt	*10 mL*
	garlic to taste	

Thaw spinach or broccoli, steam or boil, drain well and place in bowl. Saute mushrooms in a little butter and add to spinach. Stir in cheeses, beaten eggs, sour cream and seasonings. Scoop out pulp from tomatoes (and use in another vegetable dish such as Ratatouille, recipe page127). Leave 1/8"rim of pulp around insides of tomatoes. Stuff the tomatoes with the egg-cheese mixture, mounding tops. Place tomatoes in pan, bake 30 minutes or until very hot at 375ºF (190ºC).

If you wish to prepare this ahead, don't stir eggs into spinach mixture until ready to bake.

Desserts

Sugar is irresistible! On arrival, people staunchly announce their diets; then recant when they encounter the cookie bowl. I nibble at cheesecakes, pretending they're wheat germ. Despite all my nutritious resolutions, the resort loves dessert.

So I send snack bags of leftover sweets out in the boats, and tack "Baked Alaska" onto dinner.

Since the inlet landmarks bear such colorful names, I've prefaced many dessert recipes with them. No particular logic to it. I love this area, and serve it to you in many ways.

Alert Bay used to be John's home ground. It's a small fishing village where John taught in the high school and developed his boating "know how" during free time. We tied *The Aunt Molly* up at the wharf there one winter and I got acquainted with some of the Indian community and good local cooks like Audrey. She encouraged me — an anxious fledgling cook — to try pie baking. We began with this recipe...

Audrey's Lard Pastry

Makes two 9" crusts

1-2/3		
cups	all-purpose flour	425 mL
1 tsp.	baking powder	5 mL
1/2 tsp.	salt	2 mL
1/3 lb	lard (should be at room temperature)	175 g
	1 egg plus	
	enough water to make 1/3 cup total	100 mL
1/2 tsp.	vinegar	2 mL

Sift dry ingredients, into large bowl and cut in lard. In a small bowl, mix egg, vinegar and water. Beat with fork to mix, and stir into dry ingredients. Stir dough into ball. Divide ball in halves and wrap and chill each half until ready to roll out. *Or* roll out the amount you plan to use, fit into pie plate, then wrap and chill. Prick all over with fork if you're planning to pre-bake crust before adding filling.

And here's another infallible pastry recipe.

Aunt Dot's Butter Pastry

Makes one large 9 to 10" crust, or two 8" crusts

Uses softened butter; is rich, and heavier than lard pastry. Good with meat or fruit pies, or with quiches.

1½ cups	all-purpose flour	375 mL
1/2 tsp.	salt	
1/2 cup	butter (should be room temperature)	125 mL
1/4 cup	cold water	

Sift dry ingredients into large bowl. Cut in butter with *fingers* until coarse — crumbled. Stir in water and form dough into a ball. Wrap and chill until ready to use, or roll out and fit what you need into 9" or 10" pie plate. For a flakier crust, roll pastry into 9" or 10" round, fold in half and then in half again to make a "quarter." Roll out to full pie-shape, fit into plate, chill, until ready to use. If pastry needs to be partially baked before adding filling (for quiches, for example), prick all over with fork and bake.

Strawberry Fluff

Serves 4 to 6

A light, cold souffle, good with raspberries, too. Make early in day, and chill.

12 oz	one pkg. frozen sweetened strawberries (or raspberries)	340 g
1 cup	fruit juice, (add port wine to make up to this amount)	250 mL
3 oz	one pkg. strawberry "Jello" powder (or raspberry Jello for raspberry fluff)	135 g
1 Tbsp.	sugar	15 mL
1/2 cup	port wine	125 mL
2 tsp.	lemon juice	10 mL
1/2 cup	whipping cream (or frozen evaporated milk)	125 mL

Thaw fruit and reserve. Pour juice into medium saucepan and heat to boiling. Remove from heat, add Jello and sugar and stir until dissolved. Add wine and lemon juice. Chill in fridge until thick but not solid.

Meanwhile whip cream to stiff peaks and chill (or re-freeze whipped milk).

When Jello mixture is cold and thick, whip to foamy. Fold in whipped cream or milk and reserved berries. Pour into deep serving dish (6 cup or 1.5 litre size). Chill at least 2 hours until firm.

Good garnished with toasted slivered almonds, or candied mint leaves.

Ahnuhati River lies deep down the inlet, secluded, near its head. Ahnuhati seems a mysterious dark pool rather than a river. A haven for fish, bear, mink, loons and racoons. Sometimes we land guests there to pick wild blueberries, or fish for trout. They coast the glaciers and waterfalls of the inlet, then come to rest at Ahnuhati.

In May, local Indian seiners chug up the inlet, chasing the oolichan run. They sink their nets near Ahnuhati in ambush, they corral the milling fish.

This is a yearly ritual, vital to the Indian's use of and reliance on their country. Then, off they putter. Ahnuhati subsides into silence.

Ahnuhati Cold Almond Souffle

Serves 6 to 8

I enjoy the nutty airiness of this dessert. It's not crunchy. Yet the touch of toasted almonds adds depth. A cool, smooth accompaniment to heavier main dishes like Swallow Inn Steak and Kidney Pie (recipe page 110) or Northern Pizza (recipe page 116) or even Viv's Tourtiere (recipe page 113). Make early in day, then chill at least 2 hours.

2 cups	canned evaporated milk	500 mL
1/4 cup	finely-chopped almonds - toasted	75 mL
	6 to 8 slivered almonds - toasted	
1½ Tbsp.	unflavored gelatin (1½ envelopes plain gelatin)	25 mL
1/4 cup	cold water or almond or coffee liqueur	75 mL
	2 eggs	
1 cup	sugar	250 mL
1/2 tsp.	almond extract	2 mL

Early in day, freeze 1 cup (250 mL) evaporated milk until ice crystals form over the top (use a shallow, broad-mouthed bowl for this): meanwhile, toast all almonds and cool. Add gelatin to water and let stand to dissolve. Scald remaining one cup evaporated milk. Separate eggs. Lightly beat the 2 egg yolks with 1/2 cup of the sugar and the 1/4 cup chopped toasted almonds. Slowly stir the scalded milk into the yolk mix. Cook over low heat, stirring, until mixture thickens. Don't allow to boil! It'll curdle if overheated! Remove pan from heat. Stir in softened gelatin mix and almond extract. Stir well until gelatin is dissolved. Let mixture cool to room temperature.

In separate small bowl, whip the egg whites stiff. Set aside. Stiff-whip the frozen evaporated milk. Whip in the remaining 1/2 cup (125 mL) sugar. Fold white and whipped milk into cool

gelatin mix. Pour souffle into 2-quart dish. Garnish with toasted, slivered almonds.
Chill at least 2 hours.

Strawberries Jubilee

Serves 10 to 12
Recipe may be halved for 5 to 6 servings

Sailcone's version of "Cherries Jubilee." Basically fresh strawberries flambeed in brandy, then poured over vanilla ice cream. Very easy. Can be made early in day, or 1 hour before serving.

2¼ lb	ripe firm fresh strawberries	1 kg
2 cups	water	500 mL
1 cup	sugar	250 mL
1/4 tsp.	salt	2 mL
	2 liberal dashes nutmeg	
	2 liberal dashes mace	
1/2-1 tsp.	almond extract — to taste	2-5 mL
2 Tbsp.	cornstarch	30 mL
1 cup	brandy	250 mL
	one 2-litre container vanilla ice cream.	

Hull and wash berries. In large saucepan, combine the 2 cups water, 1 cup sugar, 1/4 tsp salt. Bring to boil and add berries. Cook briefly until berries *just* beginning to soften, but still firm. Remove from heat and cool. Berries will soften more as they sit. Stir in the spices and almond extract. Drain berries, reserving juice and fruit in separate containers. Measure out 2 cups of the juice and reserve any remaining juice for other use (e.g. in the "Rindy Orange Juice" in breakfast section). Make a paste by slowly adding some of the 2 cups juice to the cornstarch. Combine all the 2 cup juice with the paste and boil until thick and clear. Cool thoroughly, then stir in berries. Set saucepan containing the berries and thick syrup to one side until serving time.

At serving time, heat the berry mixture to very warm. Divide ice cream among 10 to 12 bowls and arrange on dinner table. Place hot berry mixture on table. Quickly heat the 1 cup brandy and pour it, while flaming, into the warm berries. Stir well and quickly ladle berries and syrup (they may still be flaming) over ice cream in each bowl. Serve immediately.

The winter of the fire was the winter of "Baked Alaskas." I perfected my recipes on patient Minstrel Island recipients.

This required delicate maneuvering. I prepared the basic dish at home. Then, carefully, I had to plan the transfer of Alaska, egg whites and syrup over slippery woodland trails, slowly, keeping my Alaska unmelted, to Swallow Inn's freezer. *Then* we had to rev-up the slow old propane stove in the hotel's kitchen. This took a long time So we'd wait, over beer in the parlor, for the requisite high high heat.

Finally, everyone would leave working on our lodge for the command performance. I'd whip out the chilled beaters, raise my Alaska from the depths of the freezer, lather the meringue into magnificent swirls, brown it all up in a final 4 minute burst of sweating creativity, and present the whole effort in one superb flourish, to the parlor.

Effortless Baked Alaskas

Serves 6 to 8

Really very easy. Save and freeze all your leftover egg whites for this recipe. Then thaw 3 whites on "Alaska Day" for the meringue.

Most of the work is done ahead of time: days, weeks, or at least 4 hours before serving.

Here's your choice of the boozey cake and liqueur combinations:

Chocolate — Mint: Uses Creme de Menthe syrup with chocolate cake.

Chocolate — Orange: Uses Triple Sec or Kahlua syrup with chocolate or orange cake.

Amaretto: Uses almond liqueur syrup with almond white cake.

Orange: Uses Triple Sec syrup with orange cake.

Chocolate — Coffee: Uses Kahlua or Creme de Cacao syrup with chocolate cake.

Decide which of the above combinations you wish to serve. Accordingly, make one of the following cake bases:
(recipes follow).
Orange cake, almond white cake, or chocolate cake.
Cakes can be frozen until day of the dessert. Then thaw cake and prepare matching liqueur syrup.

Orange Cake

Makes two 9" rounds.
Preheat oven 350⁰F (180⁰C) grease and flour two 9" round cake pans.

1/2 cup	butter or margarine	125 mL
1 cup	sugar	250 mL
	2 eggs — beat into the above	
1-3/4 cups	all-purpose flour	425 mL
2½ tsp.	baking powder	12 mL
½-¾ tsp.	salt	2-3 mL
2/3 cup	orange juice	175 mL

Cream butter, sugar and eggs. Beat in sifted dry ingredients alternately with orange juice - (I use a powdered mix plus water). Pour into pans. Bake 350⁰F (180° C) 20 to 30 minutes, or until tests "done" in center. Cool 10 minutes in pans on rack. Then turn out and cool thoroughly. Chill. To freeze, wrap each round separately in foil, then in plastic bag.

Almond-White Cake

Makes two 9" rounds

	2 eggs	
1½ cups	sugar	375 mL
1 Tbsp.	baking powder	15 mL
2¼ cups	cake flour or all-purpose flour	575 mL
1 tsp.	salt	5 mL
1/3 cup	oil (preferably safflower)	100 mL
1 cup	milk	250 mL
1 tsp.	vanilla extract	5 mL
1/2 tsp.	almond extract	2 mL

Separate the eggs. Place the whites in a medium bowl, the yolks in a small bowl. Reserve the yolks. Beat the whites to light foam. Into the whites, gradually beat 1/2 cup (125 mL) of the sugar, until whites form a very stiff and glossy meringue (takes 10 minutes or so). Refrigerate. Grease and flour two 9" round cake pans.

Sift into large bowl: remaining 1 cup (250 mL) of sugar and other dry ingredients. Add oil, milk, flavorings and yolks to the flour mixture and beat 2 minutes. Fold in egg whites. Pour into pans. Bake 350ºF (180ºC) 30 minutes, or until cake tests "done" in center. Cool on racks, in pans, 10 minutes. Then turn out of pans and cool thoroughly. Chill. Or freeze, wrapping each cake separately in foil, if not planning to use soon.

Chocolate Cake

Make as for white cake, above but substitute the following ingredients: — for flour, use 1-3/4 cups (425 mL) white flour and 1/2 cup (125 mL) cocoa powder. — for vanilla, use 1-1/2 tsp. (7 mL) vanilla extract and omit the almond extract.

Final Preparation:

On day you plan to serve the dessert, prepare your matching liqueur syrup. Use the liqueur that corresponds to your cake

138

and liqueur choice: either Creme de Menthe, Triple Sec, Amaretto, Kahlua, or Creme de Cacao.

Liqueur Syrup

1/2 cup	water	*125 mL*
1/4 cup	sugar	*75 mL*

In small saucepan, boil slowly for 5 to 7 minutes. Boil until syrup *starts* to thicken and caramelize. *Do not* stir! Do not let crystallize!Then remove from heat and stir in 2 Tbsp. (30 mL) of your choice of the matching liqueurs. Cool well. Should thicken more as it cools.

To Put Together The Alaska

3-4 cups	vanilla ice cream	*750 mL -1 L*
	3 egg whites (can be previously frozen)	
6 Tbsp.	sugar	*100 mL*
1/8 tsp.	cream of tartar	*1 mL*

Early in day, or at least 2 hours ahead of serving, mound ice cream on one chilled or frozen cake round. Reserve or freeze the remaining cake for another time. Leave 1" space of cake showing around edges. Dome ice cream toward center. Freeze all until firm.

Meringue

Heat oven to 450° F (230° C).

Beat egg whites to foamy: slowly beat in sugar until stiff. Then add cream of tartar. Beat until very stiff and gloss (5 minutes or longer).

Remove ice cream/cake from fridge and quickly spread meringue over ice cream and cake, swirling into peaks to seal around all edges of pie plate. Immediately place in oven. Bake 450° F. (230° C) for 4 minutes or until meringue peaks turn golden-brown. Quickly cut into 6 to 8 wedges. As you place each slice on a plate, dribble liqueur syrup over. Serve immediately.

Rum Cream

A delicious topping for almost any dessert.

1/2- 2/3 cup	whipping cream, chilled	125- 200 mL
	or	
1/2 cup	evaporated milk, frozen until ice- crystals form solidly across top (takes 1 to 2 hours) sugar to slightly sweeten rum and vanilla extracts — to taste	125 mL

Then, 30 minutes before serving, whip the cream or frozen milk to fluffy. Whip in sugar and extracts. Chill cream, or re-freeze the milk until ready to top-off dessert.

Wine-berry Meringue Dessert

Serves 6 to 8, recipe can be doubled

A light, crisp meringue pie filled with fresh fruit or straw-berries, and whipped cream.

Bake meringue the night before and leave in oven overnight.

The Meringue

	3 egg whites — may be previously frozen, then thaw the day you plan to make the meringue	
1/8 tsp.	salt	1 mL
1 cup	sugar	250 mL
1/4 tsp.	cream of tartar	1 mL
1/2 tsp.	almond extract	2 mL
1/2 tsp.	vanilla extract	2 mL
2 Tbsp.	slivered almonds	30 mL

Place whites in large, *clean,* deep bowl. Using electric mixer, beat until foamy (5 minutes or so). Beat in sugar gradually, and continue beating until whites form thick, stiff peaks (10 minutes or so). Add remaining ingredients *except* almonds and beat 5 minutes more or until stiff. Butter a 9" glass pie plate. Swirl meringue over bottom and up sides of plate (about 1/2" (1.5 cm) thick all around), sprinkle with almonds. Bake, 275°F (140° C) 1 hour, *without* opening oven door. Let dry in oven at least 3 hours, and preferably overnight. Should emerge golden and crusty. Early next day, remove meringue from oven. Place on rack. Set to one side.

Cream and Fruit Topping

15 oz	one package frozen sweetened berries (strawberry or raspberry)	*430 g*
	or	
	fresh berries or fruit — 2-3 cups (500-750 mL) — e.g. peaches, cherries, kiwi fruit, papaya *or* any combinations of these fruits	
1-1½ cups	port wine and reserved berry juice	*250-375 mL*
2 Tbsp.	(or more — to 3*Tbsp.*)cornstarch	*30 mL or more to 45 mL*
1 cup	heavy whipping cream	*250 mL*

Thaw and drain berries. Reserve the juice and berries in separate containers, *or* wash, drain and slice fresh fruit. Sweeten and set to one side. For frozen berries, add to the reserved juice enough port wine to make 1 to 1/2 cups (250-375 mL) liquid.

Into small bowl stir small amount of this liquid (1/4 - 1/2 cup or 75-125 mL). Add cornstarch. Slowly stir in remaining liquid. Pour into small saucepan. Boil to thicken. Cool thoroughly. Then add reserved berries.

Beat cream to stiff. Sweeten lightly. Spread evenly over meringue. Spread thickened berry-wine mixture (or the fresh berries or fruit) over center area of meringue and cream, leaving edge of crust uncovered. Chill at least 2 hours (or all day).

To serve: Cut "pie" in 6 to 8 wedges with thin, sharp knife (I use our curved fillet knives). Very crusty! So may be difficult to cut. Cut 5 to 10 minutes before you serve the dessert (gives you lots of time to saw slowly through the crust).

Trawlers pass our resort. People work in their worlds. Sometimes fishermen or *Service-Nine* (see salal jelly recipe) will stop off for a friendly visit, drop off our mail or a catch of prawns, look hopefully at the cookie bowl. Over hot tea, we chat. Tides, my energy, and guests, flowing, ebbing. In the corner the makings of dessert waft tempting smells...I often work as I socialise, aware of my dinner schedule geared to the tides and evening light, feeling the pressure of timed food preparation. And, if there's room, I'll invite visitors to dinner, or save them an extra-special piece of dessert.

On Pineapple Rum Cake nights, though, there are never any leftovers! Not for visitors, or Spencer the crow; not even for our guests when they boat in at 10 p.m. Nothing. It's a favorite, here.

Pineapple Rum Cake

Serves 6 to 8
Serve warm with whipped cream or Rum Cream

Pineapple Topping

1/4 cup	butter or margarine	75 mL
1/2 cup	brown sugar	125 mL
1 Tbsp.	dark rum	15 mL
19 oz	one can pineapple rings — drained	540 mL
	4 to 6 halved, drained red maraschino cherries	
	Sprinkle toasted chopped walnuts over all — optional	

Melt butter and add sugar and rum. Spread evenly over bottom of skillet. Spread pineapple slices over this and place a cherry in the center of each slice. Set aside.

The Cake

1½ cups	flour (white, whole wheat, or half 'n' half)	375 mL
2 tsp.	baking powder	10 mL
3/4 cup	sugar	200 mL
	2 eggs	
1/2 cup	soft butter or margarine	125 mL
2/3 cup	milk	200 mL
1 tsp.	fine-grated lemon rind	5 mL
1 tsp.	almond extract	5 mL

Sift dry ingredients together. In large bowl, combine eggs and butter and beat until very fluffy. In another bowl combine milk, rind and extract. Alternately stir sifted dry ingredients and the milk and extract mixture into the egg mixture. Stir well. Spread evenly over pineapple mixture in skillet. Bake 350ºF (180ºC) 45 minutes.

To serve: Remove cake from oven when done and cool on rack 5 minutes. Loosen edges with knife. Invert on large platter or cookie sheet. Cut in wedges and serve each warm topped with Rum Cream (see recipe page 140)

Hot Rum Cake

Serves 8 to 12

A warm, moist dessert-cake. Prepare 1½-2 hours before serving. Serve warm, soaked with rum glaze.

The Cake

1 cup	butter or margarine	250 mL
2 cups	sugar	500 mL
3 cups	sifted all-purpose flour	750 mL
1/2 tsp.	baking soda	3 mL
1 tsp.	salt	5 mL
	3 large eggs	
1 tsp.	vanilla	5 mL
1/2 cup	dairy sour cream	5 mL
	or make your own sour cream, using	
6 Tbsp.	evaporated milk mixed with	90 mL
2 Tbsp.	lemon juice	30 mL
1/2 cup	dark rum	125 mL
1 cup	fine-chopped walnuts	250 mL

The Glaze

1/2 cup	butter	125 mL
1 cup	sugar	250 mL
1/2 cup	dark rum	125 mL

Pre-heat oven to 325° F. (160° C.). Grease and flour 10" tube pan. Sprinkle walnuts evenly over bottom of pan. Combine all ingredients for cake in large bowl and beat 4 minutes, using electric mixer. Pour batter into pan.

Bake 325° F. (160° C.) 1 hour or longer, until tests done in middle.

Invert cake onto rack. Cool slightly until warm, then place in rimmed pan.

To prepare the glaze: Melt the butter. Add the sugar and boil 5 minutes, stirring. Add the rum and boil until syrup slightly thickened. With a large skewer, poke holes all through the warm cake and then pour glaze slowly over, until all absorbed. Spoon up any glaze from bottom of pan onto cake.

Serve cake warm.

Old John's been a hand-logger in Knight Inlet since the twenties. Originally, he emigrated from Russia, bearing an unyielding determination to forge his own life. It must have been a strange new country to him.

I never knew John very well, but I admired his 74-year wiry courage. Regularly at 7 a.m., John would steadfastly putter off to his log claim. I'd see him leaping logs, skillfully handling heavy saws and chains. An agile, determined old loner.

Though he was a meticulous, fussy housewife, John's cooking habits horrified me. He excelled at gray, boiled steak. Whenever I sneezed, he'd proclaim smoked chicken livers to remedy.

John avoided most people. Occasionally, he'd shyly express his awkward thick English in jokes. He kept his face so deadpan, I'd usually miss the punchlines.

Last year John decided to rejoin the community. I think he figured it was time to compromise. He took his stubborn individualism and independence back to Russia, to family.

I miss the sight of his trusty old yellow boat chugging around Lull Bay, and our halting discussions of John's latest toothache -his way of making contact.

To me, John represents an extreme, dying way of life on the coast. One of isolation, loneliness, and immense endurance. He went home...

Occasionally, John would allow himself dessert. He liked it simple, which this recipe is.

Old John's Pear Crisp

Serves 6, can be doubled

Easy, crunchy fruit dessert. Makes 10" pie size. Serve warm with vanilla ice cream or Rum Cream. (See page 140).

29 oz.	one can pear halves, drained (reserve juice)	1 L
1 cup	brown sugar - packed	250 mL
1 cup	white flour	250 mL
1/2 tsp.	salt	2 mL
1/2 tsp.	cinnamon	2 mL
1/2 cup	margarine or butter	125 mL
	chopped candied ginger	
	almonds (5-8 whole nuts), slivered and toasted	

Place pear halves, plus some of their juice, in greased 10" pie plate. Mix dry ingredients in small bowl and blend in butter with a fork. When dough is crumbly, spread it thickly over and around pears. Sprinkle with ginger. Bake 15 to 20 minutes at 425° F. (220° C.) until hot, and crumb top is browned. Cool on rack 5 minutes. Cut in wedges and serve each warm - with dollop of Rum Cream topping, garnished with almonds and chopped candied ginger.

For a long time we alternated fishing between Siwash Bay and Protection Point. Then a logging camp moved in to Protection and the fish left. However, I remember it as a lovely green cove as familiar as this cobbler.

Protection Point Peach Cobbler

Serves 4 to 6. Double recipe for 8.

Serve warm with Rum Cream topping. A homey, easy dessert, rich with cinnamon and Aunt Dot's biscuits.

29 oz.	one can sliced peaches, well drained	1 L
1/2 cup	brown sugar	125 mL
1 Tbsp.	flour	15 mL
1 tsp.	cinnamon	5 mL
1/4 cup	butter or margarine	75 mL

Arrange peaches in 9" glass pie plate. Combine sugar, flour and cinnamon and sprinkle our peaches. Dot with butter. Bake 425° F. (220° C.) for 15 minutes until hot and bubbling. Meantime, prepare *Aunt Dot's Shortcake Biscuits* (recipe p. 146). Drop by spoonfuls over peaches.

Return to oven to bake, 12 to 15 minutes until biscuits cooked and golden. Serve hot or warm with Rum Cream (recipe p. 140) topping off each portion. You may need to make double recipe of the Rum Cream.

Strawberry Shortcake

Serves 6 to 8

Strawberry Filling

15 oz.	2 pkg. frozen sweetened strawberries	430 g x 2
	or	
4 cups	fresh berries, half of them mashed	1 L
	to make juice	
1½ Tbsp.	cornstarch	25 mL
	liberal dash nutmeg - to taste	
1/4 tsp.	approx., cinnamon - to taste	1 mL
1/2 tsp.	approx., lemon rind - to taste	2 mL
	perhaps more sugar - if you wish	

Strain juice and reserve. Reserve berries in separate container. Combine small amount of juice with cornstarch in saucepan. Slowly stir in remaining juice, add spices, rind and sugar if desired. Heat and boil, stirring until thick. Cool completely, then add reserved berries.

Cream Cheese Filling

4-8 oz.	plain cream cheese, softened	125-250 g
	sugar to taste - not too sweet!	
	Brandy - to taste	

Whip the soft cream cheese until fluffy. Stir in sugar and brandy. Reserve.

Then make **Aunt Dot's Shortcake Biscuits**

2 cups	all-purpose (or half	500 mL
	whole wheat) flour	
1½ tsp.	cream of tartar	7 mL
1 tsp.	baking soda	5 mL
1 tsp.	salt	5 mL
2 Tbsp.	brown sugar	30 mL
6 Tbsp.	margarine or butter	90 mL
1 tsp.	fine-grated orange or lemon rind	5 mL
	dash nutmeg	
3/4-1 cup	milk	200-250 mL

Into large bowl, sift dry ingredients. Work in margarine with fingers until crumbly, add rind and nutmeg. Add milk to the flour mixture. Stir. Foil-line and grease a large cookie sheet. Drop 12 to 14 large spoonfuls of mixture on cookie sheet. Bake at 425° F. (220° C.) 12 to 15 minutes or until golden brown. Then set biscuits on rack.

To serve: 10 minutes before serving, warm the berry filling. Split hot biscuits crosswise. Butter each half with the sweetened brandied cream cheese. Pour some of the warm berry filling, (reserve half of it), over the biscuit halves. Place other biscuit halves on top. (Depending on number of people to serve, you might serve only half a biscuit per person. I usually serve a whole biscuit to each guest.) Pour remaining berry filling over top of biscuits. Top with whipped cream or double recipe of Rum Cream, (recipe p. 140). Serve immediately.

"Old folks" - many of my pals at the resort are mid-years, or older, guests. Janet I've mentioned in the "Breads" section. Then there's Jerry - lawyer/guest/friend whose taciturn stern expression belies a warm heart. Jerry earnestly cares about people. In and out of the courtroom or office, he uses an intriguing command of language to help them. People respect his quiet honesty. I cross-examine recipes with him! For Jerry's an inventive chef.

There's Rich - my pilot pal. Singing through his 60's, Rich pilots private planes for a prominent Utah machinery firm. They guest-in to fish every year, entrusting their lives to Rich. He's a master of flight...... Rich loves movement. Even writes poetry that soars. His spirit journeys freely: through the skies, on desert winds with his motorcycle, throbbing to his own drumbeat music, flowing in his poetry. Rich reveals motion in his hand-polished rocks: fluent colors imprisoned in form. Jewelry conveying the lovely moods and shades of his desert country.

Contained in his own rough form, disguised with humor, Rich's creative aliveness loosens and lightens us.

Italian Clara - a Los Angeles lady in her 70's. Energetically active (she's a *tough* fisherwoman), Clara does volunteer work for city hospitals. I suspect she spends much of her time helping sick people. Mainly, Clara makes you feel plain good. Flowery scents surround her (I fight to restrain myself from audibly sniffing! Clara smells so nice). Near Clara you find yourself grinning; a feeling of care. Clara's a clown! Makes fun of herself, mothers other guests while teasing their quirks and foibles; challenges the guys to fishing contests. All her life she's worked hard, often painfully. Clara takes time to perk people up. She enjoys her age.

Some of my older pals are American or Alberta farmers. Retired from former professions, they've slowed to enjoy work at their own pace. Other friends, like Aunt Molly (whom I've described in the breakfast section) or "Old John" (in the dessert section), stubbornly create their own unique occupations. Molly's a novelist; John hand-logs in Knight Inlet. Their work expresses their style of life. They like working.

I love our "Old Folks." They've never *really* retired from life.

Like a good dessert, "Old folks" enrich our lives....

Olde Apple Pie

Serves 6 to 8

Double recipe of Aunt Dot's Butter Pastry (page 132) or use Salmon Coulibiac pastry recipe (page 86).

6 cups	apples - preferably green and tart (usually takes 7 apples or more)	1.5 L
1 Tbsp.	fresh lemon juice	15 mL
3/4 cup	sugar, half brown and half white	200 mL
2 Tbsp.	all-purpose flour	30 mL
1/8 tsp.	salt	.5 mL
1/2 tsp.	finely-grated lemon rind	2 mL
1/4 tsp.	nutmeg	1 mL
3/4 tsp.	cinnamon	3 mL
2 Tbsp.	butter or margarine	30 mL
	1 egg - beaten	

Cut dough in half and roll out enough to line bottom of 9" pie plate. Chill. Reserve other half to roll out later.

Into large bowl, pare, core and slice medium-thin: (I use my medium-slicing Cuisinart blade for this - saves me at least 30 minutes).

To prevent apples from turning brown, keep slices covered with plastic wrap as you work. Quickly toss in lemon juice. In small bowl, combine sugar, flour, salt, rind and spices. Add the sugar mixture to apples mixture. Toss well.

Place apples in bottom of crust-lined pie plate. Mound slightly toward center. Dot with butter. Roll out top pastry, (should be thick). There may be more than you need. Fit top crust over pie plate. Flute and seal edges with fingers. Reserve extra crust for other dishes. Brush 1 beaten egg over top to glaze pastry. Then cut 3 or 4 vents (slits) in middle of top crust.

Bake, 425° F. (220° C.) for 50 minutes. Test through vents with fork to see if apples tender, and bake longer if not. You may need to put cookie sheet under pie halfway through baking, in case it starts to drip. Then remove to rack. Cool awhile before serving, giving pie time to "set."

At serving time, serve each piece of pie with a large dollop of Rum Cream (recipe p. 140) *or* vanilla ice cream on top. Yum!

Glendale, like Bones Bay, is another ghost town of the coast. The cove used to house a logging camp, gymnasium, cinema, store and post office. These buildings now lie rotting, hidden in the forest. Only the twisted pilings - remnants of a wharf into Glendale River, indicate man's presence here. By August, the humpies (mature pink salmon) return up Knight Inlet to spawn. So we send our speedboat *Georgie* to the river mouth. Humpies are fun sport to cast, although we throw most of them back.

Mainly, Glendale's a welcome change. Guests roam the riverbank, explore the old town's trails, wade the shoals. At times we've shared comic accidents: people stranded on logs by the tide, watery tumbles over embankments, scary confrontations with bears. Years later, return guests still chuckle over these incidents.

Glendale now shelters our nearest competitor - the "green boats" camp (we being the "red boats"). In honor of their friendly, funny presence, I named this recipe (my invention) after their cove.

Glendale Cove Rhubarb Pie

Audrey's Lard Pastry (recipe p. 132)

5-6 cups	frozen rhubarb pieces	1-1.5 L
	or 4 cups fresh	
1 ¼ cups	sugar	325 mL
1/4 cup	all-purpose flour	75 mL
1/2 tsp.	nutmeg	2 mL
1 Tbsp.	butter	15 mL
	2 eggs	

If using frozen rhubarb, thaw overnight or early in day. If using fresh, you'll need a little less. Reserve juice.

Make pastry (Aunt Dot's is good too, but heavier). Roll out pastry halves, fit one into pie plate, reserve the other for the top.

Chop rhubarb into 1/2 inch pieces.

Sift dry ingredients into medium bowl. Using fingers, blend in butter. Beat eggs and stir into flour mixture. Add rhubarb and juice. You may need less juice from frozen rhubarb.

Stir. Spread mixture in pie shell. Arrange remaining pastry to cover, scallop edges with fingers. Cut three vents or slashes in center. Bake 450° F. (230° C.) for 10 minutes, then reduce heat to 350° F. (180° C.) and bake 40-45 minutes more until rhubarb feels tender to fork (pierce through vents). Cool on rack and serve.

Cheesecakes are now a dinner tradition. During a five-day stay I'll make sure I serve a cheesecake. Guests are always curious to try new varieties so I'm always inventing new cheesecakes.

Banana 'N Chocolate Cheesecake

Serves 8, makes a huge 10" pie

Quite a gooey, rich dessert. The cheese part is thick and almost runny in consistency. Make early in day and chill well.

The Crust

1 cup	Graham crumbs	*250 mL*
1/4 cup	sugar	*75 mL*
1 tsp.	cinnamon	*5 mL*
1/4 cup	melted butter or margarine	*75 mL*

Combine dry ingredients in medium bowl. Stir in butter. Press into greased 10" pie plate. Press up sides. Bake, 350° F. (180° C.) for 5-10 minutes or until edges slightly browned. Cool on rack.

The Filling

8 oz. ea.	two pkg. plain cream cheese - softened	*250 g ea.*
3/4 cup	sugar	*200 mL*
	juice of 2½ small to medium lemons	
1 tsp.	vanilla	*5 mL*
	2 eggs	
	1-1½ bananas - sliced thickly	
	1 to 2 squares semi-sweet chocolate - grated	

In large bowl, beat cheese, sugar, juice, vanilla and eggs. Into cooled crust, slice bananas, sprinkle with grated chocolate and pour cheese mixture over all. Sprinkle additional grated chocolate over top of cheesecake (optional).
Bake at 325° F. (160° C.) for 20 minutes or until "set" around edges but middle still wobbles when you shake the pie. Cool on rack. Chill. Middle will "set" more in the fridge.

In this tree-covered country I'm allergic to trees, which means a reluctant monthly self-vaccination. So I combined practicality (my insulin syringes), with some fun in this recipe. Read on and you'll see the connection.

Chocolate Strawberry Cheesecake
Serves 8 or more

Really rich! Inject whole strawberries with liqueur. Dip them in chocolate, and arrange them over a fluffy, almond cheesecake. I created this dessert for a group of Nebraska farmers, of whom "Hap," "Shorty," and "Wayne" are regular returning guests and friends. They definitely approved. Make cheesecake early in day, or at least 4 hours before serving.

The Crust

1/4 cup	butter or margarine	75 mL
1 cup	Graham wafer crumbs	250 mL
1/4 cup	sugar	75 mL
1 tsp.	cinnamon	5 mL

Combine dry ingredients in medium bowl. Add the melted butter. Stir well. Press into greased 10" pie plate. Press evenly up sides. Set plate aside.

Cheese Filling

	3 eggs	
12 oz.	cream cheese	375 g
1/2 cup	sugar	125 mL
1 tsp.	vanilla	5 mL
1/2 tsp.	almond extract	2 mL

Beat cheese and sugar. Separate eggs. Slowly beat yolks into cheese mixture, then add vanilla and almond extract and beat again. Beat whites stiff and fold in to the above. Make sure you fold it all in. Pour all into Graham crust. Bake 30 minutes at 325° F. (160° C.) or until set.

Topping

1 cup	dairy sour cream	250 mL
3 Tbsp.	sugar	45 mL
1/2 tsp.	almond extract	2 mL
	Combine in small bowl.	

When cheesecake is baked, remove from oven and increase oven temperature to 450° F. (230° C.) spread sour cream topping over and return to oven for 5 minutes. Cool on rack, then chill until completely cold, at least 3 hours before serving.

Chocolate-Strawberry Topping

2 Tbsp.-		
1/4 cup	any orange liqueur *or* almond liqueur (Amaretto)	*30-75 mL*
	16 to 24 whole, large strawberries	
8 oz.	semi-sweet chocolate, chopped	*250 g*
1 cup	whipping cream chilled	*250 mL*
1/4 cup	sugar	*75 mL*
1 Tbsp.	orange liqueur, Amaretto *or* almond extract	*15 mL*

Using an insulin syringe (I buy mine at Vancouver drugstores), inject as much liqueur as each berry can hold into its center. Stand each liqueur-filled berry with injected end upright in a pie plate. Let "marinate" 30 minutes. Inject more liqueur if you think any berries can hold it.

Meanwhile, over double-boiler, melt chocolate. Stir until melted. Turn off heat and set aside.

Then whip cream to stiff, adding sugar gradually. Stir in liqueur to taste. Chill.

After 30 minutes of "marinating," dip berries (I use chopsticks or two forks to hold each berry) into melted chocolate, rolling each until completely coated. If chocolate gets too hard in pot, re-heat to melt. You may need to add and melt more chocolate if it runs out. Place each choc-berry on greased pie plate to harden. Chill.

Arrange chocolate-berries decoratively over top of cheesecake (2-3 per person) and mound a dollop of whipped cream on and among berries. Chill until serving time.

To Serve: Cut in wedges, with 2 or 3 berries atop each wedge. Optional Toppings:

Instead of strawberries, top with any fruit - blackberries, raspberries, blueberries, rhubarb. Use either canned pie filling or make your own topping by cooking the fruit and thickening with cornstarch.

This is my easiest and most embarrassing cheesecake. I confess to using canned pie filling. To my surprise it's great.

Cherry or Blueberry Cheesecake

Serves 6 to 8

Make early in day and chill.
One pastry recipe (see recipe for Audrey's Pastry, p.132 or make Graham crumb crust, recipe p. 151)

8 oz	softened cream cheese	250 g
	1 egg	
1/4 cup	sugar	75 mL
1/2 tsp.	vanilla	2 mL
2 tsp.	fresh lemon juice	10 mL
1 tsp.	fine-grated lemon rind	5 mL
19 oz	one can cherry or blueberry pie filling	540 mL
2 tsp	lemon juice	10 mL
1/2 tsp.	almond extract	2 mL
	perhaps more sugar to taste - 1/4 cup (75 mL) or less with Graham crumb crust	

Fit pastry into 9" pie plate. Beat cheese, egg, sugar, vanilla, rind, juice and blend until smooth and creamy. Set aside.

Combine pie filling, lemon juice, almond extract, optional sugar. Stir well. Pour into unbaked pastry. Spread evenly. Pour cream cheese filling over this. Swirl through the pie filling mixture until large curves of cherry or blueberry show.

Bake 35 minutes at 350⁰F (180⁰C) or until top is "set" but still a bit creamy (it'll firm up when chilled). Cool. Chill at least 2 hours.

Apple-Plum Cheesecake

Serves 6 to 8

I serve this every time Jack Wilkinson comes fishing. He loved it five years ago, talked about it every successive summer, so I finally made it a "Welcome Jack" tradition.

The Crust

1 cup	all-purpose flour	250 mL
1/4 cup	sugar	75 mL
1/2 cup	butter or margarine	125 mL

Sift flour and sugar into medium bowl. Blend butter in with fingers into a dough. Grease 9" pie plate. Press dough over plate bottom and evenly up sides. Bake 20 minutes at 350ºF (180ºC) or until gold-brown.

Filling

14 oz	one can applesauce	398 mL
1/2 tsp.	cinnamon	2 mL
8 oz	cream cheese	250 g
	2 egg yolks (reserve whites)	
1/4 cup	sugar	75 mL
1/2 tsp.	vanilla	2 mL

Mix applesauce and cinnamon. When crust is baked, spread applesauce mix over, bake 350ºF (180ºC) for 10 minutes. Meanwhile beat cheese, egg yolks, sugar and vanilla. In a separate bowl beat egg whites until stiff. Fold into the cream cheese mixture. Spread over the baked applesauce and bake 20 to 25 minutes, or until cheese is just set. Cook on rack.

Plum Glaze

14 oz	one can purple plums	398 mL
1 Tbsp.	cornstarch	15 mL
3 Tbsp.	sugar	45 mL
	reserved plum juice	
1/4-1/2 tsp	almond extract — to taste	1-2 mL

Drain plums and reserve juice. Slice plums in half, discard stones, drain plum halves on paper towels. In a small saucepan mix cornstarch and sugar with 1/4 cup (75 mL) reserved juice. Stir into this 1/2 cup more plum juice (or add port wine, if not enough). Boil until thick and clear (1 to 2 minutes). Add extract. Cool thoroughly.

When cheesecake and glaze are cold, arrange drained plum-halves over top of cheesecake in a "flower-petal" design. Spoon all glaze over and spread evenly. Chill until serving time, then cut in wedges (try to have a plum on each wedge). Quite hard to cut through the crunchy crust, so I usually cut dessert just before I serve dinner. Saves last-minute hacking and hewing!

Mrs. Moses has never visited *Sailcone*. She operates her own friendly version of the resort in... Los Angeles! When I attended a conference at her camp, I was delighted to encounter the same hospitality, care, and personal cooking so natural to coast communities. Mrs. Moses radiated simple warm strength. Through the L.A. rains and mud, through my morning jogs past sumptuous Santa Monica homes, Mrs. Moses' unobstrusive presence made me "at home." L.A. and the inlet now both feel welcoming. Mrs. Moses has transformed L.A. into "Santa Monica *Sailcone*" for me.

I haunted Mrs. Moses' recipe collection and returned with this cake.

Mrs. Moses' Carrot Cake

Makes a 9" x 13" cake

The best carrot cake! Moist with pineapple and coconut and nuts.

2 cups	all purpose flour	500 mL
1½ cups	sugar	375 mL
1 tsp.	baking soda	5 mL
2 tsp.	cinnamon	10 mL
1 tsp.	salt	5 mL
2 cups	finely grated carrots	500 mL
1 cup	coarsely chopped walnuts (or pecans)	250 mL
1 cup	flaked coconut	250 mL
8 oz	1 can crushed pineapple	220 mL
	3 eggs	
1/2 cup	vegetable oil	125 mL
2 tsp.	vanilla extract	10 mL
3/4 cup	buttermilk (I use regular or powdered milk and add 2 tbsp (30 mL) white vinegar or lemon juice, then more milk — enough to make the 3/4 cup (200 mL) of liquid)	200 mL

Sift dry ingredients into a large bowl. Beat the eggs, oil, vanilla and buttermilk together, then beat into dry ingredients. Mix well. Stir in carrots, pineapple, walnuts and coconut. Pour evenly into greased, floured 9x13" pan. Bake 350⁰F (180⁰C) for 35-45 minutes or until done in the middle.

Toppings

You have three choices here.

Mrs. Moses Hot Buttermilk Syrup

2/3 cup	sugar	225 mL
1/4 tsp.	baking soda	1 mL
1/4 cup	butter	75 mL
1/3 cup	buttermilk	100 mL
	(I use canned evaporated milk and scant lemon juice)	
2 tsp.	light corn syrup	10 mL
1/2 tsp.	vanilla extract	2 mL

Combine in saucepan, bring to boil and stir over medium heat, boiling, for 5 minutes. Remove from heat. Add vanilla.

Prick surface of hot cake with fork and pour hot sauce over it. Leave in pan to cool. Serve in squares.

Cream Cheese Frosting (my favorite)

3 oz	cream cheese	100 g
1/4 cup	butter or margarine	75 mL
1¼ tsp	grated lemon peel	7 mL
2¼ cups	icing sugar	575 mL
	rum extract - to taste	

In medium bowl, beat together the cheese, butter, peel and sifted icing sugar until fluffy. When cake is completely cool, spread frosting evenly and serve cake in large squares.

Rich Rum Sauce

Very thick and sweet. A superb sauce to pour over ice cream too.

1 cup	evaporated milk	250 mL
	(essential don't use cream)	
1 cup	sugar	250 mL
1 cup	butter	250 mL
4 tsp.	artificial rum extract	20 mL
	dash salt	

Combine ingredients in saucepan and bring to boil, stirring until thickened (5 to 10 minutes). Sauce thickens more when cooled. Pour some sauce over each serving of cake, or pass sauce and let guests help themselves.

For nine years, John and I have operated *Sailcone*. We've changed with the resort. A golden pine lodge — built with our sweat and Minstrel community's help; a hot tub out on the wharf; a growing fleet of small boats; the *Georgie* — John's cherished speed boat. We freighted in a 10 kilowatt generator and finally, after overcoming my suspicions, added my valorous dishwasher.

We've welcomed the machinery. In many ways, it's freed us.

Our "busywork" is lighter. We relax more with the guests. Even my pace has slowed. Increasingly, I connect my work with nature.

We weren't sure this tough country would accept us. Nine years later, we're confident of our lifestyle. We've ripened.

Friendships now ripple to various cities. And city people flight in to blend with us. Increasingly, I involve myself in the city —Vancouver. Growing a sense of "family" not confined in the inlet or coast.

Sailcone is a miniature casserole of coast life. People converge, stir their different characters, get lost in the "pot," and usually choose to stick together. Knight Inlet provides a beautiful setting to nourish our selves, and each other.

Index